Channeling Your
Passions

Channeling Your Passions

Cedric B. Johnson, Ph.D.

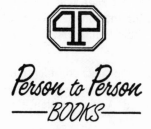

Person to Person BOOKS

Palm Desert, California / Dallas, Texas

Person to Person
——BOOKS——

Palm Desert, CA
92261-3229

Channeling Your Passions

Copyright © 1985 by Cedric B. Johnson

ISBN 0-933973-02-0

Scripture references, unless otherwise specified, are from the
Holy Bible: New International Version, Copyright © 1978 by
the New York International Bible Society. Used by permission
of Zondervan Bible Publishers.

Author's Note: To protect confidentiality, the names and iden-
tifying details in the case histories reported within this book
have been changed. Any resemblance to persons living or dead
is purely coincidental.

Printed in the United States of America

Contents

The Streams of Human Nature

The Streams of Human Nature

You are a passionate person. Now that may be the best kept secret in the world. "Still waters run deep" could well apply to the expression of your emotions. On the other hand, your problem may be that you wear your feelings on your sleeve. Such a free expression of emotion gets you into difficult situations. How do you find balance in the expression of passion?

As human beings, we have to learn to live with our passion, our strong feelings. As Christians, we search for the place of passion in the walk of faith. Some churches help their people freely express passion. Tears, hugs, ecstatic utterances, and strong desires are freely expressed. Other congregations are more formal in the expression of their faith. The emphasis is on rationality. Where is the truth to be found for balanced Christian living? How are we to express our passion?

Passion is a strong word. Passion in love and adventure, an empassioned plea, passion fruit, and compassion all connote the exotic and extreme. Can such a term be used to describe aspects of the Christian life? Dare we allow passion to guide us through the challenges of life?

This book is written for Christians, like myself, who sometimes feel confused about strong desires that well up within them.

Yet, the Bible's pages are full of the expression of powerful feelings—from the Father's exhuberance over his creation, and his grief over the condition of fallen people, to the celebration of heaven's angels at the birth of Jesus. In addition, the full gamut of human emotions are recorded from Genesis to Revelation. The apostle James, for instance, credits fights between people to the "passions at war in your members," but then assures us that Elijah was a person "subject to like passions as we are" and when he prayed fervently, it rained.

Human nature is made up of two basic streams. Along the riverbed of our humanity flow the streams of sinfulness and life. The dark stream of sin leads to spiritual and emotional death. It is like some of the underground rivers in Death Valley, California that contain dangerous and poisonous materials. Persons who drink such water become violently ill and sometimes die. The stream of life flows from the heart of God through the lives of all His children. The water brings life like a clean and sparkling mountain stream. The riverbed of human nature is ever changing and sometimes very fragile. At times the hurts of life act like a flood that causes the river to break its banks. The destructive power of hurt is manifested in unchanneled passion and shattered human relationships.

Using the text of John 13:33–14:7, we will study the

impact of these two streams as they flowed along the bed of Peter's humanity. We will see how his passions and abilities flowed in both a dark as well as a light stream. Our journey toward wholeness in Christ must involve an honest insight into the two streams in our own lives. We then need to find ongoing healing in the One who dealt with our stream of sinfulness on the cross and rose again that we may participate in his stream of life.

The Stream of Sinfulness

We cannot hope to experience wholeness in our passions until we take an honest look at our dark stream. The goal of our journey into the stream of sin is not despair but deliverance. We must heed the advice of St. Augustine and love the sinner but hate the sin. First, we will study the part of us that often pushes "panic buttons" as it did with the apostle Paul who cried out, "What a wretched man I am! Who will rescue me from this body of death?" (Romans 7:24). Then we will look at the One "on whom our iniquities were laid" and see the divine answer to the stream of death.

The apostle Peter, with characteristic zeal and candor, looked Jesus in the eye and boasted, "I will lay down my life for you," (John 13:37). But less than twenty-four hours later, frustrated and confused, Peter slipped off into the shadowy Passover morning and wept bitterly. He had not only broken his promise, but he had also denied his Lord. The stream of tears that flowed from his eyes had its source in the river of sin. His uncontrolled passion serves as a warning of similar tendencies in our own lives. We don't need preachers to tell us that we are sinners. Most of us painfully identify with the words of the apostle Paul, "For what I do is not the good I want to do; no, the evil I do not want to do—this I keep on doing," (Romans 7:19).

We all need to become acquainted with the negative part of our person that the Bible calls sinfulness. In some ways we cannot stand the sight of this part of our person. We push it into the unconscious part of our minds and thereby feel that we have disposed of it. This is not true. We simply have given it permission to have automatic control over our behavior. The river of sin springs up unexpectedly in human relationships in the form of prejudice, blame and hostility.

We need to face the stark and fearful reality of the depths of our sinfulness even after we become Christians. We dare not let ourselves become overconfident like Peter who boasted that he would never betray his Master. We are warned by the apostle Paul, "So, if you think that you are standing firm, be careful that you don't fall!" (1 Corinthians 10:12).

Fortunately for us, sinfulness is not the last word on our human condition. Peter was forgiven and restored in his relationship with Jesus. We will consider ways to deal with the river of sin in our lives later in this chapter. We now consider a river that impacts our lives for good.

The River of Life

The riverbed of our humanity also carries a life-giving stream. The river finds its source in the heart of the Lord and flows through the lives of his children. Jesus spoke of this river when he said:

> If a man is thirsty, let him come to me and drink. Whoever believes in me, as the Scripture has said, streams of living water will flow from within him.
>
> (John 7:37–38)

The words "within him" refer to the seat of human passion. There are times when our strong feelings reflect the character of God. There were many times when this river of life flowed through Peter. For example, one day Jesus asked his disciples to give him feedback from the public opinion polls of his day. "Who do people say the Son of Man is?" said Jesus. Peter replied that he was the Messiah. Jesus then told Peter that the source of the confession was God himself. Matthew 16:13–17) The stream of life was evident in Peter's impulsiveness that day.

There are times when our lives touch others in a life-giving manner. A smile, encouraging word, hug, or an artistic gift to the world are a few examples of the river of life. Even the most wicked person shows this river at some time. It is reported that certain Nazi death camp leaders would go home from their evil work to tenderly play with their children and animals. There really is "honor amongst thieves." The river of life may be reduced to a mere trickle but it is there despite monumental human wickedness. A personal faith experience in Christ ("If any man thirst let him come to me and drink.") restores the flow of the river of life and sends the river of death into the sea of God's forgetfulness.

Traces of the river of death, however, are always evident in our lives. We need to come to terms with the presence of our dark stream. We also need to find ways to ensure the flow of the river of life in our thoughts, passions, and behavior. First, however, we need to map out the riverbed of our humanity.

Human Frailty

The terrain through which a river flows is changeable and very fragile. Flood conditions, types of soil, and the slope of the ground are some factors that affect the nature of the riverbed. In a similar manner, our humanity is frail, changing, and susceptible to environmental changes. Sometimes Peter was unaware of the frailty of his humanity.

When Peter boasted of his self-sacrificing loyalty, Jesus gently questioned him, "Will you lay down your life for me?" The Master then gave Peter a more realistic picture of what would occur in the following hours. He said, "I tell you the truth, before the rooster crows, you will disown me three times!" (John 13:38).

What Peter needed then was insight—not only into himself and his needs, but also into the difficult situation that lay ahead. Because of his humanness, Peter was not capable of looking into the future and realizing the stress he would experience. Perhaps if Peter had had more insight into his own character he would not have denied his Lord. He obviously did not recall passages of Scripture that speak of the transient and frail nature of human power and ability like this one:

> All men are like grass,
>   and all their glory is like the
>   flowers of the field . . .
> The grass withers and the flowers fall,
>   but the word of our God stands
>   forever.
>
> (Isaiah 40:6–8)

Similarly, many times we fail because we don't know our human limitations and inclinations. Or, we may not have accurately anticipated the demands of a given situation. Our ability to predict the future is just too limited.

A story is told about a motorist who followed a large truck up a winding, mountain road. Over and over again, the frustrated driver tried to pass the slow-moving truck, only to be stopped by an inability to see what lay beyond the next curve. Far above the two vehicles, a pilot in a small airplane observed the scene. "If only I had some way to talk to the driver of that car down there," he thought, "I could tell him when it would be safe to pass the truck."

The man in the plane had a bigger picture of the situation than did the motorist, whose view was obscured by the next bend in the highway. The motorist needed a broader perspective which couldn't be gained from his vantage point. How often we find ourselves in similar circumstances. We weave and dodge our way through life, struggling with our limited ability to anticipate what's coming next. If only there had been a way for the person in the plane to communicate with the driver. In our situation, on the other hand, God has ways to tell us about our limited perspective in life. He provides adequate guidance in his Word to help us with patience or provide a way of escape from the obstacles of life. We are told in the Scriptures:

> No temptation has seized you except what is common to man. And God is faithful; he will not let you be tempted beyond what you can bear. But when you are tempted, he will also provide a way out so that you can stand up under it.
>
> (1 Corinthians 10:13)

What we lack sometimes is insight into the limited perspective of our humanity as well as trust in the God who sees the whole picture. We must recognize our human frailty. We need wisdom, patience, and trust in the management of our energy and perspective. Jesus set the example for us as a human being who needed rest, solitude, and time alone with God.

We must take into account the fact that our humanness can become the occasion for sin. We are often overwhelmed by the river of sin in our moments of exhaustion and discouragement. In unguarded moments of stress the "street angel" becomes the "home devil" as we hurt the very ones we love. No wonder then that Peter went out into the night and wept bitterly. He still had much to learn about himself, human frailty, trust in God. He also had to find more productive ways to deal with the hurts and disappointments of life.

The Flood of Hurt

There is no doubt that Peter deeply disappointed himself when he failed his Master. We read that he went into the night and wept bitterly. Like all of us he experienced the loneliness of sorrow. It seemed as though all the tears in the world could not wash away the stain of his guilt. However, we need to note that these were the tears of godly sorrow that led him into the experience of being restored and forgiven. He shed the healing tears of which the apostle Paul wrote, "Godly sorrow brings repentance that leads to salvation and leaves no regret, but worldly sorrow brings death," (2 Corinthians 7:10).

Very seldom are the hurts of life resolved as quickly as Peter's. Within the span of a few days he was restored in his relationship with Jesus. Some of us carry the legacy of years of hurt. As a psychologist, the chief area of hurt that I deal with in my own life and that of my patients relates in some way or another to rejection.

One of the greatest hurts of life is the experience of rejection by our parents. Sometimes the pain is so great that we push it into our unconscious minds in the futile attempt to resolve the hurt. We even speak wistfully of our "perfect" childhood and deny the rejection.

Who then are these people who have experienced rejection? A few examples may help you identify a similar wound in your heart. Children of alcoholics or workoholics have experienced emotional and physical abandonment which is interpreted, "I must have been a terrible person if my parents did not want to take note of my existence." Others have been hurt by physical and sexual abuse. These early hurts are compounded by the normal rejections we feel in adolescence where certain friends come in and out of our lives with alarming inconsistency. The wounds become deeper as we get older even though we feel that we are becoming tougher in the face of rejection.

We have some very strange ways of trying to compensate for rejection. Some of us become chronic people pleasers. We try to be perfect in all that we do and so win approval. Others of us become very suspicious in relationships. Their watchword is that nobody can be trusted—including God. The bottom line is that unresolved hurts from the past render us ineffective in our relationships with others. In a sense, it was easy for Peter to recover from his hurt. It did not fester in his heart for many years. What then do we do with our hurts? The answer is contained in our response to both the river of life as well as the river of sin in our lives—through insight and through action.

Insight

We need insight to discover fresh ways to be honest about the hurt and darkness within. We also need courage to own our own strengths. But where does this insight come from? Peter received the direct confrontation of Christ who let him know that he had miscalculated in his thinking. In the absence of Christ's visible and audible presence with us, who or what is there to remind us of our river of sin, our hurts, and our river of life?

Insight into the sinful and hurt portions of our lives comes only after our walls of defense have fallen. We work hard for long years to build systems of denial. The way to health and the full and free flow of the river of life is through dealing honestly with these defenses. Let us now consider ways that we can peek behind our defensive walls.

Sometimes all that is required for insight is to have a caring friend help us articulate our deepest feeling. Think of a situation that you refuse to face but still brings you anxiety. Can you fill in the blanks in the following sentence? "I feel _____ because _____, and I want _____." Simply going through this exercise, alone or with a friend, can help you identify what you are experiencing. Consider the example of Al who constantly relived the pain of his abandonment by his parents. The scars of this hurt from the past left him afraid of intimacy. His struggle, when he came to me for counselling, was whether he should make a marriage commitment. In the past he had been described by women in his life as "attractive but aloof." As we wrestled with the hurts of his past, he was eventually able to admit how deeply he felt the pain of abandonment. His admission was:

> *I feel* threatened,
>   *Because* I don't want to be abandoned again,
>   *And I want* to learn to trust people again
>   because I feel such loneliness.

Another source of insight can be the input of friends who care enough to confront us in a loving way when they sense that something is wrong. Jesus looked Peter in the eye and said, "You are not going to lay down your life for me, Peter. You are going to deny that you even know me." In the same way, honest feedback from friends can sometimes alert us to areas of sin, frailty, and hurt in our lives.

A third source of insight can be a more comprehensive understanding of human nature on our part. The Bible, recounting the lives of persons "subject to like passions as we are," can be the window to our hurt or sinful selves. (Great literature and art and the reflections of the depth psychologies can also lead us into a better understanding of the self.) The apostle Paul wrote of the Scriptures, "For everything that was written in the past was written to teach us, so that through endurance and the encouragement of the Scriptures we might have hope," (Romans 15:4). The Bible provides us with hope for the future, because it tells of a gracious God who responds to our dark stream and our hurts.

I often find that I become mildly depressed after I view the local and national news. I once had a television news anchorperson tell me that he quit his job because he hated reporting sensational stories of the baser human instincts. Stories of rape, domestic violence, war, terrorism, murder and robberies push up the ratings of the show but depress the human spirit. The story of the Bible is, "But where sin increased, grace increased all the more," (Romans 5:20).

With such sources of insight we need to move on to responsible action. Certain constructive behaviors and attitudes can help us deal with the stream of sinfulness flowing along the riverbed of our hurt humanity.

Action

We tend to run scared in the face of the negative aspects of the self. The lesson of faith is that we engage our "hold" buttons before we hit the "panic" buttons.

Don't Panic

Our first course of action is to keep calm. Jesus, in his wisdom, had just set Peter straight as to the way he would behave in the coming hours. He predicts Peter's failure, and in the next short breath, says, "Let not your heart be troubled" (John 14:1). Our Savior understands the troubled person. He knows that the person who focuses on the dark stream of human nature can become confused and panicked. A herd of cattle in a similar state stampedes without a sense of direction. Likewise, a troubled heart runs into emotional disability. Peter wept. Judas hanged himself. Yet, Jesus encountered the dark stream without panic.

Perhaps you are thinking that the statement, "Don't panic" is an impossible way for you to respond to your own struggles in life. Let's examine several sources of panic that may help you to change that opinion.

The Accuser. Satan is called "the accuser of the brothers." (Revelation 12:10) He loves to come before God and our consciences, pointing his finger at our human shortcomings. "How can you be a child of God when you . . ." he will whisper. We listen to him and become fearful and anxious. We forget that his is not the constructive, convicting voice of the Holy Spirit that leads us to repentance (2 Corinthians 7:10), but the voice that drives us to frustration, despair and sin.

The Idealistic Self-Image. Sometimes we set ourselves up for a panic situation by focusing on the value of our performance, rather than on the value of our person. We conclude that we must be competent and achieving to be worthwhile. We feed on panic-producing statements of an "if—then" nature. For example, I might say to myself, *"If* I do not publish this book, *then* I will not be considered a scholar," or *"If* I am late to this meeting, *then* people will think I am irresponsible."

Each of us has some of these "if—then" statements which influence the way we view ourselves. They form a sort of target image—a standard of performance by which we judge our successes and failures. Falling short of this image can lead to panic.

Paying the Consequences. Sin ultimately produces painful consequences. The apostle Paul gave the Galatians a good lesson on this principle when he said:

> Do not be deceived; God cannot be mocked; a
> man reaps what he sows. The one who sows to
> please his own sinful nature, from that nature
> will reap destruction; the one who sows to
> please the Spirit, from the Spirit will reap
> eternal life."
>
> (Galatians 6:7–8)

At times, each of us is faced with the consequences of our stream of weakness. We may panic at our sinful tendencies and hide ourselves from God and others. We may have denied our hurt for years and the first insights may cause great personal anguish. We need not panic. It is unnecessary to run from ourselves. The same Lord who said to Peter, "Let not your heart be troubled," urges us to believe that he can salvage us at our weakest moments. He calls all strugglers to faith.

Trust God

The second course of action that helps us deal with our human frailty, hurt, and sin is to be found in Jesus' words, "Believe in God, believe also in me," and "I go to prepare a place for you." This is the opposite of panic, and the perfect complement to Jesus' instruction, "Let not your heart be troubled." The only reason we can resist the voice of the accuser, and the fear of the consequences of the dark stream in our lives, is that we have a trustworthy God. In him we are secure, regardless of our shortcomings.

Some of you may respond, "It's all very well for you to tell me to trust God. I have tried those formulas so many times that they become empty words for me." Let me assure you that I also have a distaste for easy solutions, because they have not worked for me or for any of my patients. The experience of trusting God is more than the magical repetition of Christianized mantras like "I am trusting God." Faith is more than a superstition. It is the response of the whole person to the God who reveals himself in his Word. It is our responsibility to keep our eyes open to the many sources of his revelation.

We can also trust him because he has experienced the full force of both our hurt as well as our darkness. He

bore our pain in his own body on the cross. The writer
to the Hebrews tells us:

> We do not have a high priest who is unable to
> sympathize with our weaknesses, but we have
> one who has been tempted in every way, just as
> we are—yet was without sin.
>
> (Hebrews 4:15)

Somehow it helps for us to know that our friend Jesus
has faced all the hurts of humankind. Think for a moment of all your experiences of rejection. Then contem-
plate the rejections of Christ. He was "despised and rejected of men," forsaken, denied, and betrayed. He then
experienced the ultimate rejection, that of God, as we
hear his painful cry on the cross "My God, my God, why
have you forsaken me?" He can truly say to each of us in
our hurt, "I understand." It helps to have a personal
friend who understands our struggles.

To have understanding for our pain and sin is one
thing; to have a solution is another. Jesus told the disciples that he was "going to prepare a place" for them.
When he spoke of a "place," he was not just speaking of
heaven. His mission in life was to provide a solution for
our river of sinfulness and hurt. Jesus prepared a place
for us at Easter. Potentially we can be free of the vice-
like grip of our evil and hurt. The full flow of the river of
life can be released in our lives because "blood and
water" flowed from his side. We can begin to be all that
God intended us to be because of Jesus. We can find our
place in this world because he took our place on the
cross.

A Personal Life Response

What is the worst thing you have done in your life? Has Christ forgiven you for that sin and failure? Have you forgiven yourself? Do you feel forgiven or do you allow the enemy to accuse and intimidate you about it?

What is the worst hurt that you have experienced? Is it possible for you now to take that hurt to Jesus? Try the following exercise:

Close your eyes in a moment of prayerful meditation. Think of Christ on the cross. Imagine that you are leading a small child on a tour of the hill called Calvary. The child represents you and your long forgotten hurts. Point the child to the dying Jesus on the cross. As your gaze alternates between the child and Jesus imagine the pain of the child being transferred to Jesus. Continue the process until your hurt is literally absorbed by the dying Christ. Now imagine Resurrection Sunday. Imagine a carefree child romping hand in hand with the risen Christ. Feel his risen life in your heart of hearts.

Applying the Truth

- Think of a situation about which you hurt. Then fill in the blanks as follows: "I feel _____, because _____, and I want _____." Try to identify your precise feelings and needs in the specific situation.
- Seek the counsel of a friend whom you trust, or a counselor who has a good reputation, and work through areas of sin and hurt. Also find ways to

discover the river of life in you as expressed in your gifts, works, and abilities.

- Memorize and meditate on John 14:1–6, especially as it relates to your particular situation. In what ways can the content of the verses keep you from panicking over failure, hurt, and sin?
- Consider the relevance of James 3:10–12 to the various parts of your person.

Do You Want to Get Well?

What Do You Think?

Sometimes people hurt in life because they are afraid of health.	Yes	No	Maybe
Most emotional/physical/spiritual healings are sudden.	Yes	No	Maybe
The only way we hear the voice of the Lord is through the Bible.	Yes	No	Maybe
Being the person God intended me to be involves risk and suffering.	Yes	No	Maybe

Do You Want to Get Well?

Throughout my life I have encountered many bogus cures for the emotional and physical hurts of humankind. I remember with chagrin a patient of mine suffering from a multiple personality who had to resist attempts by Christian friends to cast demons out of her. Their ministrations were based on good intentions but a faulty diagnosis of the situation. In other instances, the prescribed cure is based on local superstition. Many years ago I served as a short-term missionary in South America. During my term of service I contracted a severe bout of influenza. One of the local people suggested that I wrap myself in a wet bedsheet and sleep that way for the night. It was believed that such a procedure would cure my ailment! The man at the pool of Bethesda believed with all his heart in a long-held tradition. (John 5:1–15) Every year there would be a subterranean movement in the pool which the people believed to be caused by the action of an angel. The first one in the pool would be cured.

Sometimes the pain of human suffering makes us run in the direction of relatively ineffective cures. Like the man at the pool, we have to find our cure in an encounter with reality as it is revealed in the Man of Galilee. As we consider together this healing event we will see how many false cures actually serve to increase our personal misery. For example, take the abused wife who is told by her pastor that the solution for domestic violence is unbending submission to her husband. Consider the severely depressed person who is told that the cure is more faith in the Lord. I am alarmed how often such misinformed solutions are presented to people today. In the face of such malpractice, we need to focus on the John 5:1–15 portion of Scripture which sets forth certain principles that help cure these "cures".

Insight

Accurate diagnosis is an important step in an effective healing event. Alcoholics Anonymous recognizes this. Each person, using his or her first name, must introduce himself or herself, saying "Hello, my name is Joe and I am an alcoholic." We are often slow to admit our personal responsibility in reversing our problem situation. The man at the pool had learned to be helpless. Consider his pitiful response to Jesus' question, "Do you want to get well?" "Sir, I have no one to help me into the pool when the water is stirred." The reasons for his hopeless state were both social and personal.

Many times we are trapped in our pain by a set of social circumstances. The man at the pool of Bethesda was caught in the socially accepted belief that an angel moved the water once a year.

Recently I saw a cartoon in a local newspaper that stereotypes the plight of the poor. Two members of the present administration were depicted as riding in their limousine through a poor district of Washington, D.C. One said to the other, "It's a pity these people don't want to be rich like us!" As long as it is a socially accepted belief that poor people are poor through their personal choice, we will wait for a cure for such social ills. Just as the belief in the healing powers of the pool of Bethesda kept hundreds of people trapped in their sickness, so the myths of widespread welfare cheating and minimal hunger in our country contribute to the poverty of many now.

People are also trapped by the disability of the human spirit. Thirty-eight years of physical disability had crushed this man's hope of a cure. He had adapted to the role of being an invalid. Certain human adaptations to disability are healthy. Helen Keller learned effective human communication skills despite her disability. She accepted the reality of her physical limitations but refused to be crushed by them. The spirit of the man at the pool was a stark contrast to that of Helen Keller. So, Jesus asked him, "Do you want to get well?" We all need a person like the Man of Galilee to motivate us towards health.

The sheer selfishness of humankind was another reason the man was hopeless. He was trapped by "The Rule of the Pool" which, put in other words, was everyone for themselves. I can hardly imagine one person saying to another, "After you," on the day the water moved. It is more conceivable that there was a mad scramble in which people were trampled on and hurt.

The reasons presented so far for the man's helplessness are: social myths, human selfishness, and adaptation of the human spirit to the sick role. But these were not greater than the power of Jesus.

Encounter

The word and person of our Lord are available to deliver us from the power of our crippling human predicaments. His gentle invitation to health is spoken all the time, but we do not hear the healing voice. Each day the air is filled with thousands of seeds seeking a place to germinate and grow. The hard ground of our hearts and the thorns of concern about material things prevent the seed of the Word from having an impact in our lives. How do we hear his voice, obey, and find deliverance like the man in the pool?

In the first place, we don't have to acquire a complete knowledge of Jesus before we experience the impact of his power. The man at the pool did not have a clue as to the true identity of his benefactor. In our Westernized society, the acquisition of facts is seen as the way towards wholeness and personal power.

Yet, our healing encounter with Christ does not always have to be based on logical reasons. The special prayer language used by many Christians is evidence that God can be experienced in a world beyond reason. Such prayer intimacy is almost like the preverbal contact between parent and child. The two don't speak to each other but there is a deep awareness of the presence of the other. Now before I am accused of propounding some existentialist heresy of Christianity, let me assert the importance of logic and reason in the experience of Christ. The human brain has two hemispheres which constantly interact with each other. The one deals mainly with analytical categories and the other mainly with intuitions and feelings. We are to love the Lord with our whole brain and person. However, like the man at the pool, we don't need a complete knowledge of him before we are healed.

Whenever Jesus had a healing encounter with a person he challenged them towards action. In the next section we will see how "faith without works is dead."

Action

I vividly remember one occasion when I offered a group of patients a money back cure for their emotional distress. I did not divulge the nature of the cure although it was in accordance with scientifically established methods. However, I made clear to the group of people that three things were required for participation in the program. First, they would have to be absolutely honest in reporting on their progress. Next, they would have to stay with the program for six months. Finally, they would have to demonstrate to me that they wanted to be well. The key to the success of the program was in the latter condition, the desire to be well. A few people took me up on my offer and were indeed cured from some bad habit patterns.

Jesus asked the man, "Do you want to get well?" The invitation of Jesus was filled with authority. It gave the man a will to health. The healing consisted of a partnership between God's power and the person's will to live. It is a well-known fact that seriously ill persons survive better if they have hope. The word of the Lord gives us hope. Again and again we are reminded that "Apart from me you can do nothing," (John 15:5).

The seemingly pointless question "Do you want to get well?" was a call to the sick person to take responsibility for his life. I often wonder why any person, especially one with healing resources, does not want to get well. Sometimes we view the cost of wellness as greater than the cost of sickness. Jesus viewed it the other way around. He called people to discipleship and said, "My yoke is easy and my burden is light." There is a burden and a yoke of discipline in following him, but it is far less in its magnitude than those hurts of living apart from God.

Jesus called the man to action in two ways that helped effect his cure. First, he instructed him to "Get up, pick up your mat and walk." A passive helplessness and a cure do not go together. Later, Jesus said to him, "See, you are well again. Stop sinning or something worse may happen to you." A call to morality was part of the cure. What did Jesus mean when he told the man to stop sinning?

He certainly did not imply that the man's original sickness had been caused by some personal act of sin. He was talking about the person's present state. The Master also did not specify what sin would lead the man into greater distress. I want to suggest an interpretation that expands on the statement in Romans 3:23, "For all have sinned and fall short of the glory of God." Since each one of us has the glory of God stamped on our lives, we fall short of this glory when we fall short of our potential as people. The evidence of such a "falling short" is seen in our fragmented relationships, personal loneliness, and lack of purpose in our lives. The greatest tragedy for us is that we live out of harmony with the Lord and his glory that is stamped on our lives.

Consider the example of the man who presented himself for counselling at our clinic in a state of deep depression. His first words to me were "I am the son of Dr. So and So," (a well-known personality). He felt hopeless and helpless because he could never live up to his father's greatness. Everywhere he went he was introduced as "the son of Dr. So and So." He was falling short of the glory of God in his own life by trying to define himself in terms of another person. Part of the treatment was getting him to see that he was a person in his own right. The glory of his person was quite distinct from that of his father's. I encouraged him towards the discovery of self-respect as a prelude to true worship of God and effective human functioning. The Lord challenges each of us towards the realization of his glory in us. He gives us the right to be ourselves. We need the courage to take the risk. Such courage avoids all bogus, "quick fix" cures. It involves suffering, but avoiding the realization of our potential involves greater suffering.

The name *Bethesda* means "house of mercy." However, the invalid man only found true mercy in the encounter with Jesus. The fruits of mercy became his only when he took action, first of all, by wanting to be made well. Our past ends the moment we meet the Master. We take our first steps into emotional, physical, and spiritual health when we heed his call to take up our bed and walk. For the man at the pool, the bed was a reed mat. For you and me, it could be a depressed helplessness, or seeing ourselves as a victim—of circumstances, of the rejections and hurts of the past, or of economic and political limitations.

The changes in our lives that come from obedience may not be as sudden and dramatic as those seen in the man at the pool. I often tell patients with deep-seated difficulties that their lives will not turn around suddenly like the turning of a speedboat. Rather, change will come like the turning of an ocean liner, slowly but deliberately. In the day of "quick fix" solutions, we need to heed the word of the apostle Paul who sees us changing "from one degree of glory to another," (2 Corinthians 3:18—RSV).

A Personal Life Response

Examine some of the areas in your own life where you fall short of the glory of God in your person. Are you trying to be someone else? Someone once said "An oak tree brings glory to God by being an oak tree." In your partial failure to live up to your potential:

- Are you more concerned about pleasing others than being yourself?
- Do you even have a beginning awareness of the potential of your person?

- What hurts of the past keep you from healthy living?
- Is your search for "quick fix" cures keeping you from the path of true discipleship that involves both joy and suffering?
- What are some of the possible reasons for your not wanting to get well?
- When did you last experience a merciful personal encounter with the Lord?

Applying the Truth

Take time away from your busy schedule and get alone with the Lord in a quiet place. Consider a time of retreat in a place of quiet and beauty and let the Lord speak to you through nature. Consider the trees, flowers, hills, birds, and animals. They don't spend their time straining to *do* things. They are pleasing to God in being what they *are*. Consider the pleasure you will bring to God and yourself by your simply being what He created you to be. You are "accepted in the beloved," you don't have to strain at pleasing God. Rest in his mercy and work with new energies for his glory.

The Passion for Power

What Do You Think?

Submission and power are incompatible for the Christian.	Yes	No	Maybe
It is impossible to be a servant in our competitive society.	Yes	No	Maybe
A servant can never be assertive.	Yes	No	Maybe
The church needs a "chain of command" in order to function effectively.	Yes	No	Maybe

The Passion for Power

When I first saw the television show "Dallas", I found myself fascinated by the character of J. R. Ewing. A closer examination of my passion for the program revealed that I had a latent desire to have his power. I discovered that I was like the disciples who sat around debating which of them was considered to be the greatest. In my passion for power I wanted to be the top dog who has control over other people. But then I read Luke 22.

The Passion for Power

The scene was the upper room. Jesus and the disciples were celebrating the Jewish feast of the Passover. It was Jesus' last supper. Luke gives us a glimpse of the more seamy side of the followers of the Man of Galilee. They were jockeying for position and power in the earthly kingdom they thought Jesus was going to establish. Jesus was quick to rebuke them. He told them they were behaving like "the kings of the Gentiles" who "lord it over" their subjects and "call themselves Benefactors."

(Luke 22:25) Some modern equivalents to these power plays of the "lords" of the Gentiles are found in our hearts, the church, and the world around us. We now examine the interpersonal style of these power brokers.

The Victimizer and the Victim

In most of the dramas of life there are two central characters, the victimizer and the victim. Sometimes the victimizers are individuals. Other times they are sociopolitical structures. When Jesus spoke of the "lords" he was referring to the victimizers in our midst. Our minds race to try and identify these dark characters. Maybe he is speaking of the right wing dictatorships of the world that oppress and disenfranchise the poor and helpless— the Hitlers and Stalins of the world. But Jesus was not speaking to the Roman oppressors or the corrupt religious leaders of his day. He was speaking to a group of faithful disciples, his church and his body.

The church has also been party to the passion for power of the "lords." It has supported slavery, massaged evil systems of government, kept women out of the mainstream of its leadership, and been more partial towards the rich than the poor. Religious organizations have become "worldly", seeking the approval of the "lords." Church groups become more concerned for their vested interests than for truth and the value of the individual. As part of these systems we are implicated.

Each one of us has the tendency to "lord" it over others. I often work with people who have deep scars from the past from parental domination. At times parents try to live out their unfulfilled ambition through their children. As a result the children are denied the opportunity to become what God created them to be. I vividly remember a young artist who came for counselling. He seemed to suffer from a guilt-driven anxiety whenever he practiced his artistic trade. A detailed history revealed that his father wanted him to become a physician. The parent had grown up in the Great Depression and never had the opportunity to go to college. He vowed that his children would go to college and never suffer from poverty. When the young man revealed his artistic ambitions, his father told him, "No son of mine is going to be a starving artist. Art is play and borders on frivolity. You will go to college and be a physician or some other high earning professional." He lorded it over the boy by withdrawing financial support and by constantly complaining about the waste of time of his art. The boy had to find the courage to be himself. First, however, he had to give himself his God-given right to develop and use his gift of art.

The Wool Over the Eyes

Good con artists not only oppress others but make their victims feel that they are doing them a favor. Jesus said of the "lords" that they "call themselves Benefactors."

Certain religious television personalities may well fall into the category of Christianized con artists. Television has the tendency to make all its central participants "larger than life." Some of them literally cash in on this magnifying trend. Their visions, prayers, and concerns come across as having greater efficacy than those of the mostly passive viewer. Emotional appeals centering on explosive subjects like abortion, physical and emotional sickness, capital punishment, and other social issues become the means of financial gain. Followers send money and the "lords" tell them, "We are doing this for your own good."

Now the "lords" don't have to be just media people. Husbands have twisted biblical "submission" to reinforce their need for domination. Women are told that the "chain of command" is for their own good. Blacks in South Africa are told that the system of apartheid is for their benefit. Children are told that the brutal beating given to them by their parent is "to help build your character." "But you are not to be like that," Jesus said.

The Master and Power

Jesus presents himself as a dramatic contrast to the "lords." The footwashing scene in the upper room was the occasion of a lesson on the power of servanthood. (John 13) When the disciples entered the room for the feast, there were no servants present to wash the feet of the weary travelers. They sat at table with dirty feet. Jesus took on the role of the servant and washed their feet. What a lesson the disciples learned that day.

The Defeat of the Lords

We miss the lesson of the footwashing incident if we see it only as an example of humility. Note the symbolic impact of the washing on Peter. (John 13:6–9) Note that

Jesus behaved in this way to "show them the full extent of his love" (v. 1). Consider also a passage like Colossians 2:13–15 where the cross is seen as the defeat of the "powers" or "lords." The footwashing incident was the Suffering Servant's way of declaring his defeat of the powers. In a dramatic way, like the Lord's Supper, Jesus was teaching the disciples the meaning of his death.

It is sometimes difficult to believe that the systems of oppression in this present world were defeated by the event on the "old rugged cross." We can possibly see how the cross changes individual lives but systems of evil power are less likely to change. It is here that we need to review the lessons of history. Lincoln did make a difference to the system of slavery. Martin Luther King did impact a nationwide civil rights movement. There is an erroneous belief abroad, especially in Christian circles, that "you can't change city hall." And so we keep silent in the face of evil and concentrate on individual salvation. We will see in the next section how the power of the Suffering Servant brings change to even the most evil systems of the world and in the church. The "lords" have indeed been defeated.

The Power of Servanthood

It is inconceivable to some that a servant can have an impact on the evil systems of power. Yet, the way of the cross is the way of servanthood. What exactly then is a servant? In the biblical sense it is certainly not someone in a position of weakness. Jesus acted as a servant on the eve of his crucifixion from a position of strength. Look at John 13:3 and what it says about Jesus' strong sense of identity and mission. He was able to be a servant because of an inner sense of security.

The power of servanthood is that it is a voluntary action on the part of the person. Jesus was under no constraint to wash the disciples' feet. It was a choice on his part that motivated servanthood. One application of servanthood is Ephesians 5:21, "Submit to one another out of reverence for Christ."

The apostle Paul comments on a wide range of human relationships. The power from such relationships comes from the fullness of the Spirit of God and mutual submission. It is not a command for submission but a call to voluntary submission. The key, then, is that the person who submits participates in the decision to submit. The ultimate display of servanthood was Jesus' voluntary submission to death on the cross. Now he desires a servant spirit on the part of his followers. It is in fact the best antidote for a passion for power.

The Servant and the Lords

How then can a disciple of the Master live in this day and age when the "lords" of the Gentiles are so prevalent in the world and the church? The following are some of the practical applications of John 13:17: "Now that you know these things, you will be blessed if you do them."

An Unconscious Response

The footwashing incident can be misinterpreted. Jesus was not telling his disciples "If you want promotion in the kingdom or want to become a great leader, then first behave like a servant." Servants don't consciously seek power and influence. They work the works of the Lord without an eye on the fruit of their action. Now if I were writing this section in a true servant spirit, I would not be thinking to myself "I wonder whether people will accept what I am saying" or "I hope this book becomes a best seller." Rather, I would be more concerned with being the best writer within my ability and focusing on the task in the here and now. The spirit of the servant is reflected in the surprise at the commendation of Jesus in the heavenly rewards ceremony:

> Lord, when did we see you hungry and feed you, or thirsty and give you something to drink? When did we see you a stranger and invite you in, or needing clothes and clothe you? When did we see you sick or in prison and go to visit you?
> (Matthew 25:37–39)

The behavior of these servants had not been contrived to gain the approval of either God or their fellow human beings. The "left hand did not know what the right hand was doing." True servants do not measure their worth by their accomplishments. Servant actors do not aim for stardom and Oscars but for the joy of practicing their art. Servant preachers do not crave for the adulation of big congregations but fidelity to their Lord and his Word. We must be content to go through life without watching ourselves live. The true servant lives without the agenda of being great. John the Baptist had the perspective of servanthood when he said of Jesus "He must become greater; I must become less," (John 3:30).

An Unselfish Response

It is more natural for the servant to give than to receive. The servant focuses on the best interests of the other. One of the other majestic passages of Scripture that deals with servanthood is the second chapter of Philippians. Here the writer encourages all who would emulate the Master not to look to their own interests but the interests of the other. It is common for people to ask "What do I get out of the situation?" in both work and relationships. The way of the Suffering Servant is different. The focus is on the interests of the other. Jesus said in Luke 22:26, "The greatest among you should be like the youngest, and the one who rules like the one who serves." The verse is not intended to diminish the value of the individual. It speaks against the "me first" tendency especially in relationship to the quest for and exercise of power. The servant makes a conscious effort not to emulate the "lords." Unselfishness is a position of great strength in the kingdom of God. It shows that the servant has brought the passion for power under control. Servants rest in the fact that power belongs to the Lord. They don't have to manipulate people because "God works for the good of those who love him," (Romans 8:28). They don't play the game of the power brokers because one day "at the name of Jesus every knee should bow," (Philippians 2:10). Servants have restful hearts but they can also be activists on behalf of their Lord.

An Active Obedience

Jesus did not passively endure the reign of the "lords."
The cross was his way of defeating their power. We, as
servants, are now expected to testify to the world of
power, by our actions and words, of the coming of the
rule of God into the world. We are to make a concerted
effort to stand against the "principalities and powers" in
the strength and victory of the Lord. The servant church
has a prophetic role towards political, religious, and intellectual structures that oppress people. Sin in systems
must be dealt with just as much as sin in the individual
heart.

I often become aware of the sin of the system when I
treat individuals psychologically. Often people come
into counselling in a state of deep distress. After a period
of time their emotions and behavior stabilize and they
become more productive. They then return to their fami-
lies, or jobs, or missions assignment and within a short
span of time they are in distress again. The sick and oppressive system continues to play a large part in their
mental ill-health. I have seen creative and godly missionaries destroyed by controlling supervisors or fellow
missionaries.

We must be careful of what one of my friends calls the
"sweet bye and bye" syndrome. Here we look to the
return of Christ and the end of the age as the time that
justice will come into the world. Others make the mis-
take of seeking to correct violence with violence. The
final danger is to treat the "lords" with moral prescriptions. We won't change the power structures of the

"kings of the Gentiles," inside and outside of the church, by reinstating the death penalty. Prayer in public schools will not dethrone the powers. The radical obedience and example of the church is our only chance to affirm the victory already won by the Suffering Servant. The love we have for one another, expressed in communities that transcend racial, age, and sex boundaries, is the way of witnessing to the power of servanthood.

A Personal Life Response

In what parts of your life are you hungry for power? Do you tend to "lord it over" others? Where can your presence and that of your church make a diference to the "powers?"

Applying the Truth

- What are your options as a Christian when someone "lords it over" you?
- Can you identify someone who behaves like a servant? What are the reasons for your conclusion?
- How have you been party to a misinterpretation and misapplication of submission?
- To what degree does a quest for power represent compensation for a personal sense of inadequacy?

Betrayed

What Do You Think?

Judas was destined to betray Jesus and was not fully responsible for his act.	Yes	No	Maybe
Sometimes our strengths become our weaknesses.	Yes	No	Maybe
If we love those who betray us they will repent.	Yes	No	Maybe

Betrayed

Julius Caesar looked stunned when his friend Brutus threatened to assassinate him. He cried out in anguish "Et tu Brute!" Most of us have felt the knife of betrayal plunge deep in our hearts at some time in our lives. We identify with the confused feelings of Caesar. We feel something of the anguish of Jesus as he was kissed in betrayal by his disciple Judas. We too cry out in anguish to our friend or family member "And you Brutus!" as the realization of betrayal sinks into our fogged over memories. What exactly is a betrayal? What feelings go on inside our hearts when we are betrayed? We will examine these questions with reference to the life of Judas.

Betrayed or Opposed?

How do we identify betrayal in our lives? First, we need to make a distinction between betrayal and opposition. Sometimes a parent will cry out in grief "I have been betrayed" when the child chooses a career contrary to the parental wish, or chooses a marriage partner, church membership, or personal values other than those sanctioned by the family. The rules of the family have been broken, along with the hearts of the parents, but has this been a case of betrayal?

Before we can classify an act as one of betrayal, there needs to be a violation of a higher set of principles than the wishes of a parent or society. *Betrayal is when a person works actively against the best interests of the other.* There are divine laws that define the exact nature of a person's best interests. A betrayal occurs when such a law is broken. For example, one of the commandments is "Thou shalt not commit adultery." A married man who sleeps with another woman violates the best interests of his marriage bond and thus betrays his wife. When, however, he has intellectual needs met by scholarly interaction with another woman, his wife may feel threatened and insecure, but she has not been betrayed.

There is no question, though, that Judas betrayed his Master. He sold out his Lord for thirty pieces of silver and his own agenda, and he certainly did not understand the best interests of Jesus. Judas' betrayal was not a "spur of the moment" reaction. The seeds of betrayal had been sown much earlier by the Evil One in the soil of both Judas' hurt and his giftedness.

My Strength and My Hurt Is My Weakness

When Judas turned his Master over to the religious and political leaders, it was a premeditated act. We can only make assumptions about his change from faithful disciple to turncoat. Jesus knew his heart from the beginning. From early on he predicted that one of the disciples "had a devil in him." We are not sure as to the exact meaning of that phrase, however it is certain that Judas opened himself to the Evil One when he did not deal with the disappointment in his heart. And Judas was greatly disappointed when Jesus did not fulfill an agenda of political power and influence. So, Judas was tempted where he was most vulnerable. Satan loves to mount the steed of our hurts, dig in his spurs, and watch us gallop out of control to our destruction.

The Evil One also tempts us at the point of our giftedness. Judas was the treasurer of the band of disciples. He must have had management gifts. But, his overconcern for the finances of the band of disciples caused him to miss the wonder of the occasion when the woman anointed the feet of Jesus with costly ointment. All he could think of was the price of the ointment and how it was being wasted. After all, he rationalized, it could have been sold and the money given to the poor.

We don't often consider that our strengths may well be our weaknesses. A conscientious person may become compulsive. A giving person may take too much responsibility for others. An open hearted person may become gullible. A discerning person may become skeptical. We need to beware that the place of our strength does not become the stage on which Satan acts out his evil drama.

Betrayed by the Ones We Love

The disciples did not have the slightest notion that one of their number would betray the Lord. It is difficult to believe that Judas was in their midst for three years and none of them predicted his behavior. Evidently, he had hidden his dark stream well behind the mask of faithful discipleship. When he went out into the night to perform his evil deed, the rest of the disciples thought that he was on a mission of charity. How is it that acts of betrayal lurk behind the masks of respectability? Maybe, like the disciples, we:

> ... don't take into account each person's
> propensity towards evil
> ... wear masks of religion to cover the deceit
> in our hearts
> ... allow our doubt of God's plan to become
> the seedbed of betrayal
> ... try to protect the reputation or memory of
> the loved one who betrayed us.

I recall the case of Maude who had been sexually abused by her father during her early childhood. She was very depressed when she came to me for counselling in her early thirties. She had a happy marriage and healthy children, but she was experiencing serious sexual difficulties. During our first interview, she reviewed her childhood as "perfect." She was "Daddy's little girl." After six months of counselling she began to have bothersome sexual dreams. The dreams were the means of prying open a "can of worms": incest. All these years she had protected herself from the memory. Even though the thought that her father had betrayed her innocence was almost overwhelming, she did not want to lose his approval. So she lived as if it had happened to another person. The process of healing began when she admitted the truth to herself and to her parents. It was an agonizing process to deal with her betrayal, but the truth of her past and the truth of forgiveness in Christ was part of her healing. It is one of the most difficult things in life to admit that we have been betrayed by the ones we love.

What happens when we are the betrayer, the loved one who hurts another? Before we become too critical of Judas, we need to note the possibility of betrayal in each of us. The mere suggestion by Jesus that one of their number would betray him aroused the disciples' insecure chorus "Is it I?" Did not they all forsake him and flee? Was not Peter's denial of the Master akin to an act of betrayal? The most productive thing we can do is to admit to ourselves and then to our victim that we have commited a wrong. We need to seek their forgiveness, as well as God's. We need to be realistic enough to allow them their rage and anger. At first, we will become outcasts in their eyes as they work through their grief over the betrayal. Over a period of time, reconciliation may take place. The truth of walking in the light of reality and forgiveness may then come our way. Have no illusions about the fact that the way back from betrayal is a long hard road. Jesus walked the path himself. He can provide the means of healing. Consider how he responded to Judas.

Responses to Betrayal

Leonardo de Vinci's painting "The Last Supper" is a masterpiece in the world of art. It is not accurate, however, in terms of the biblical record. The disciples were not sitting in an upright position at the table. They were reclining, as was the custom, on low couches with each person's head on his neighbor's chest. Judas was reclining to the right of Jesus so the Master was resting his head on the betrayer's chest. It was in this context that Jesus made his appeal of love to Judas.

One of the responses we make towards someone who betrays us is hurt that finds its expression in anger and acts of vengeance. We don't read about Jesus' anger towards Judas. We only see the act of forgiveness when he handed Judas the choice piece of meat. Such an act was understood in that culture as the host of the feast bestowing favor on the guest. In the same way, while we were in the act of betraying God, Jesus' death on the cross was God's choice morsel to us.

A modern illustration of such love for one's betrayer is found in Central America, where rulers are wont to torture their political opponents. After a change in government, one political prisoner became a cabinet minister in the new government. When he returned to the prison from which he had been liberated, he encountered one of his former tormentors, now a prisoner himself. In an act of Christian forgiveness which astounded the whole country, he released the prisoner and restored him to the favored position of free citizenship. The test of our Christian faith is whether we can sincerely forgive our enemies even as God has forgiven us our trespasses. People, however, do reject such love.

We all like a story with a happy ending. We all want a favorable outcome for our acts of love. Yet, there was no happy ending for the story of Jesus and Judas. Jesus showed him favor. Judas went out into the night and hanged himself. Somehow, we live with the fantasy that if we are kind and loving towards people they will make a turn towards the good. But loving people who do the will of God get betrayed by their disciples, denied by their friends, and crucified by their enemies. Where then do we get the idea that the world is a fair place rewarding good and punishing evil? Such a fantasy only will become a reality in the afterlife, in the new heaven and the new earth. The lion will not lie down with the lamb in this age. Despite the inconsistencies of this life, we can rest in the fact that the "Judge of all the earth will do right." We can, through the grace of the Lord, forgive the Judas in our lives. We do not need to hang onto unforgiveness to punish our betrayer. We can protect ourselves from the victimizer in our lives in ways other than through our anger. We can leave the matter in God's hands and be free and protected at the same time. Of course, we don't have to open ourselves to further victimization. We can exercise protective caution. Jesus did tell us to be "as wise as serpents and as harmless as doves." Sometimes we need the wisdom acquired in the "school of snakes" to be assertive, confrontive, and firm with our victimizers. We also need ways to be true to our feelings. How then do we deal with the feelings of being betrayed?

The Feelings of the Betrayed

Jesus was able to pray for his tormentors, "Father, forgive them for they know not what they do." He bore the pain of their hate and misunderstanding. He did not bear the added pain of a spirit of unforgiveness. He was able to forgive Judas. Before we forgive, however, we need to realize the extent of the hurt and hate in our hearts.

The greatest hurt in betrayal comes from realizing that we have lost a precious relationship. We go through the natural waves of grief—anger, denial, numbness of heart, and finally acceptance. The important thing is that we allow ourselves these varied feelings. We do ourselves a favor if we confide in a friend who listens, without judging us, to our confused and painful cries. It also helps greatly to share our feelings with others who have been betrayed. When we hear their stories we don't feel quite as alone in our own rage or denial. It is especially important to remember that, in uncovering the hurt of a betrayal, we need to "make haste slowly."

We let go of our hurt through the process of forgiveness. None of us are professional forgivers. God is the only one who forgives well. We usually bungle our way through the process, but, by God's enabling, we can reach the point where we wish the person well. It would be ideal if we could be reconciled with the betrayer, however, forgiveness does not necessarily lead to reconciliation. Jesus was not reconciled with Judas nor the persons he forgave while he was on the cross. Forgiveness is for our benefit. It removes the pain from our hearts. We can live again after the stab in the back by our friend. It is not the end of the world for us. It need not be so either for the betrayer.

The alternative to forgiveness is a hard and heavy heart. Being rejected by people we love often makes us defensive and lonely. We isolate ourselves in our pain and then live behind our shell for fear of intimacy and further hurt. The road through forgiveness is very difficult, then, since the pain of reconciliation seems to outweigh that of loneliness. The way back to trusting relationships is slow and involves courageous risks. Thankfully, healing can be helped by caring people who accept us and nurse us back into healthy relationships. The broken hearted need not end up in the isolation of despair. Judas is not our only model of ways to deal with failure.

Not Destined to Hang

I sometimes have the privilege of treating in psychotherapy persons who have inflicted the pain of betrayal on their loved ones. As I see their process of repentance and restoration, I am convinced that Judas did not need to commit suicide. He, too, could have found the forgiveness seen in the experience of Peter. No deed of betrayal is beyond the mercy of God. Jesus bore that betrayal in his own body on Calvary. It is because of him that we can live again. The road back to restoration is long and hard but it always goes by way of the cross.

A Personal Life Response

Consider your options if you have betrayed one of your loved ones. You can be destroyed through worldly grief or be restored through godly repentance. (2 Corinthians 7:10) Admit to yourself, God, and the person that you have sinned against them. Be prepared to face your victim's rage. Seek forgiveness and allow the process to take time.

Can you respond with grace and favor towards the betrayer in your life? Go back to John 13 and identify with the feelings and behavior of Jesus towards Judas. By what process can you come to forgive your "Judas" without opening yourself to further victimization?

Applying the Truth

- Make a list of the persons in your life who you feel have betrayed you. Be as specific as you can about the exact nature of the betrayal. Recognize however, that your emotional defense systems will only reveal to you the truth that you can bear.
- Pray for those who have used you. (Matthew 5:44)
- Examine the degree to which you hold to the "fair world" view of life. Does confronting and forgiving your victimizer restore the fantasy of your "happy" childhood. Does it insure reconciliation or even understanding from your betrayer? Be prepared for a massive denial on their part as one possible response.
- If you have been a "Judas" to a loved one, reflect how your strengths or gifts became your weakness.
- Take an honest inventory of how you have betrayed your loved one. Try and listen, without being defensive, to their confrontation of your behavior. Don't put them on trial and make it sound like their problem. The kindest thing you can do for yourself and

them is to "walk in the light." Seek forgiveness from God and the victim. Finally, forgive yourself.

- Consider the ways you are valued by God in contrast to the devaluating of betrayal.

The Many Faces of Doubt

What Do You Think?

God condemns all forms of doubt.	Yes	No	Maybe
God expects us to have all the facts straight before we act in doing his will.	Yes	No	Maybe
Doubt can lead to unbelief.	Yes	No	Maybe

The Many Faces of Doubt

Thomas has received a lot of bad press over the years. The label "doubting Thomas" has become a synonym for unbelief. We are quick to condemn the man for his lack of faith in the Master. We are slow to empathize with his turbulent passion as he tried to sort out his feelings in relationship to Jesus. Doubt acts like a strong wind that stirs up the waves of our emotion. On the eve of the crucifixion, Thomas found himself in a storm greater than any he had encountered on the sea of Galilee. His ship of emotional and spiritual stability nearly sank.

Throughout the history of the church, doubters have been treated as heretics to be burned at the stake, agnostics to be feared, nonconformists to be shunned, and freethinkers to be avoided as nuisances who "corrupt the youth." As a result we hardly ever see doubters as persons at the cutting edge of theological thought or their doubt as the shadow of faith. If we are really honest with ourselves, we will see that there have been times when we have doubted some aspect of our relationship with

God. Such doubt need not necessarily be a negative part of our growth. Some of the greatest personal discoveries have come after a period of doubt. Thomas is a key example of doubter turned believer. What then are the processes that motivate the doubter to become a believer? Under what conditions do doubting people become unbelievers? The answers will come as we explore the volatile passion of doubt in our own lives and that of Thomas. (John 20:24–31).

The Profile of a Doubter

Certain circumstances almost guarantee doubt. Most of us suffer the pangs of doubt—when we face suffering, when we are confused by self-identity questions, and when we have to remain in the dark in perplexing situations.

Suffering

As a pastor and psychologist, one of the more frequent questions I am asked is "Why do God's people suffer?" In the face of the enigmas of life "why" is not just an academic question. It is the cry of the breaking heart trying to make sense out of a senseless world. Thomas had such a dilemma. The happy band of disciples was about to have a period of great suffering. The Master predicted death for himself and Thomas intuitively knew that it was not an empty prophecy. In an expression of raw courage he said, "Let us also go, that we may die with him," (John 11:16). Soon, however, his stable confidence was to be badly shaken by an earth-quake of doubt.

Too many times we have been shaken by an encounter with painful events. We may not have come close to the experience of Job's wife who told her husband to "curse God and die," but we have cried out, "Where was God when I needed him?" Suffering can make doubters out of brave people.

Passages

One of the characteristics of adolescence is that the young person places a premium on thinking for himself or herself. Yet, we parents tend to panic when our child says defiantly, "You can't make me go to church and you can't force religion down my throat." It is easy to overreact to such a statement and engage in a power struggle that seems to divide the whole family. We need to realize that we take the risk of maturity—of needing to accept their failures and mistakes—when we encourage young people to think for themselves.

Thomas expressed their questioning spirit when he said, "Unless I see I will not believe." There is something special about his absolute refusal to believe unless he saw the evidence for himself. He did not want a second-hand faith. He refused to say that he believed when he did not have the conviction in his heart. The poet Tennyson put the struggle of doubt succinctly when he wrote, "There lives more faith in honest doubt, Believe me, than in half the creeds."

The honest, although sometimes irrational, doubt of the adolescent is an attempt to find a faith that is personal. Sometimes the identity crisis of the teenager is delayed until the person leaves the home base. It is not uncommon for first-year college or seminary students to go through a period of painful doubt. In some ways, such struggles are not the broad road to atheism but passages to the narrow road of maturity.

Uncertainty

All of us, at some time or another, have wished that we owned a crystal ball that could help us see the future. The fascination of some Christians with the biblical teaching of the end times has led to some rather unbiblical speculations. There is certainly a place in our lives for the "blessed hope" of the second coming of Christ but the desire to know the exact program for the future arises out of our insecurity. Thomas' doubt arose out of his insecure feelings because he could not know all the details of the future with the Master. Jesus had predicted that he was going to prepare a place for all his disciples. He said in John 14:4, "You know the way to the place where I am going."

Jesus' statement was too much for Thomas. He was a detail oriented person who was not willing to deal with the ambiguities of the future. He wanted Jesus to get to the bottom line. "Lord, we don't know where you are going, so how can we know the way?" He wanted details. It was very difficult for him to tolerate gaps in his knowledge.

In another example of this insecurity, we see Thomas demanding concrete evidence that his master was still not in the tomb: "Unless I see the nail marks in his hands . . ." (John 20:25). For him, seeing was believing and he could not believe unless he had as many details as possible.

God does not give us a detailed map of the Christian life. Like Thomas, we make demands of Jesus: "Tell us where you are going and then we will trust you with the details of the present." Yet, the call to faith is a commitment to a person rather than the assurance of all the details of the journey. Not all of Thomas' doubt, however, was from insecurity.

A Desire for Faith

"Unless I see the nail marks in his hands . . . I will not believe it." These are very strong words indicating an intense desire for faith. A double negative in the original language conveys the impression "I will in no wise believe it." Many times a strong statement in one direction indicates an equally strong desire in the opposite direction. Thomas was really crying out from the bottom of his heart, "I really want to believe, so please give me some evidence."

He wanted a sign that Jesus was really risen. Jesus honored his desire and appeared some days later. We know that Jesus refused to give signs to those who operated out of ill will towards him. The religious leaders asked for a sign and he did not oblige them. The Devil tempted him to give a sign by jumping from the pinnacle of the temple and miraculously surviving. Jesus rebuked him and refused. Thomas doubted, but his heart was in the right place.

There are many shades of doubt. Not all of them are

acts of rebellion against God. Some are due to our short-sightedness in suffering, others arise in the attempt to think for ourselves, some from the uncertainties of the future, and finally, some from an intense desire for faith. We will examine how Jesus responds to the needs of the doubting heart.

The Prescription for Doubt

Sometimes honest doubt leads to surprising revelations. On one occasion that Thomas expressed his doubt, Jesus made a remarkable statement. He declared that he was the "way, the truth, and the life." On another occasion, he appeared to the doubting disciple and as a result we hear the profound confession, "My Lord and my God."

Not an Ending But a Process

In the case of Thomas, his confession of faith was not an ending to the story but a point of transition. The process resulted in many years of service for his Master, culminating in missionary work in the far reaches of the earth with people of another culture. The upper room revelation was probably not the last time Thomas doubted. The answers and experiences of the past do not guarantee a life free from the struggles of doubt. The way we knew God yesterday does not always suffice for the challenges of today. We truly need to implore the One who is the Bread of Life to "Give us our daily bread."

Not All the Light but Some

I once heard a theologian say that God judges people on the light that they have received. In most cases, we don't even act on the light that we have. Again and again, the Scriptures commend people who step out into life on the basis of the light that they possess:

> Though you have not seen him you love him.
> (1 Peter 1:8)
> Blessed are those who have not seen and yet
> have believed.
> (John 20:29)

Now the Scriptures do not speak of faith as a leap in the dark, but, rather, as a journey. The way out of dark doubt involves a purposeful and continuous movement as we are drawn to the light, Jesus himself. Like Thomas, we may have a vague concept of our destination, but Jesus reveals himself to us with the assurance that he is "the way, the truth, and the life."

Not Vague Answers but God

It is not clever theological arguments that resolve the dilemmas of doubt. God did not meet the need of suffering Job with a set of theological answers. The need of Job's heart was met by God himself. Job responded to him by saying "My ears had heard of you but now my eyes have seen you," (Job 42:5).

God comes to us with a surprising freshness at the point of our need. He meets the doubting adolescent not with the canned answers of previous generations but with a fresh revelation of himself. He comes to the suffering saint not with cliches of comfort but with the Comforter. To the doubting disciple who said, "Unless I see in his hands the mark of the nails," Jesus responded, "See my hands." To Thomas who said, "How can we know the way?" Jesus responded, "I am the way."

There are times when we experience dryness in our spiritual experience. It seems that the old ways of knowing God in the midst of our doubts are no longer effective. We cry out in agony "Where is the Lord when I am in need. Is he sleeping?"

The problem is not that the Lord is sleeping in the boat in the midst of the storm. It is rather that our ability to respond to his presence is somewhat jaded by the hurts and mysteries of life. At the point of our spiritual staleness he still meets the need of our hearts, however, we may need to hear him on other channels of communication.

Not One Channel but Many

Recently I went on a personal retreat to replenish my spiritual resources. I asked a pastor friend if there were fresh ways of seeing the Lord in my life. The old method of having a "quiet time" in the morning with the study of Scripture had not been very effective at that time in my life. I asked him "What do I have to do on a spiritual retreat?" His answer was simple. "You do nothing; let your mind be quiet, consider the flowers, trees, and other aspects of God's world. God will speak to you." At first, it was difficult to shut out the clutter from my mind. The cares of the world were truly choking out the

Word of God in my heart. After an hour or so my mind quieted down. A miracle occurred. Suddenly God started speaking to me with the voice of nature, just as David had experienced:

> The heavens declare the glory of God;
>   the skies proclaim the work of his hands.
> Day after day they pour forth speech;
>   night after night they display knowledge.
> (Psalm 19:1–2)

God has all sorts of messages for us. Sometimes we need to find fresh channels of communication. I know of one man who imagines that Jesus is sitting in the passenger seat of his car. He converses with him in a very personal manner. If the heavens seem as brass when we pray, maybe we need to let God approach us through nature. (Such a revelation should always harmonize with the view of God in the Scriptures.) Jesus pointed to the care of God for the birds as an example of God's care for his children. (Matthew 6:26) The order in the universe points to God's purposeful and gracious involvement in our lives. The immense stellar systems speak of the greatness of the Lord. We too can hear his voice in the heavens and the earth.

Doubt Dispelled

The revelation of God to the doubter demands a response. Thomas cried out in a new discovery of faith, "My Lord and my God." He saw his Master in a new and life-giving manner. The sunshine of the love of Jesus caused the mists of his doubt to evaporate. But, we do not always respond with faith to the presence of the Lord. Remember that there were two thieves on the crosses next to Jesus. They both saw the same evidence. Only one received the assurance "Today thou shalt be with me in paradise." The other thief mocked Jesus all the way to his death. Doubt is the shadow of faith. It can also be the darkness of unbelief. We can choose the path of infidelity or faith.

A Personal Life Response

Reflect on the times when you have doubted God. Did the Lord strike you down with a bolt of lightning? Did you learn new things about God? Did you eventually feel closer to him? Maybe you are still in the mists of doubt. Why don't you consider listening to God on other channels?

Applying the Truth

- How can you better assist someone who comes to you with doubts about their faith?
- Why is it that God does not give us complete and detailed answers to our doubting questions?
- What do you think about the possibility of hearing God in nature?

Hatred: The Tale of Two Brothers

What Do You Think?

Our hatred has its roots in the hurtful actions of others.	Yes	No	Maybe
It is difficult to hate family members.	Yes	No	Maybe
Only time cures feelings of hatred.	Yes	No	Maybe
The cure for hatred is forgiveness.	Yes	No	Maybe

The Tale of Two Brothers

All of us with brothers and sisters have competed with them in one way or another. Sometimes the competition leads to productive behavior. In the case of Cain and Abel, it led to murder. (Genesis 4:1–16)

The killing of Abel was not a spur of the moment act. It had a history deep in Cain's psyche. It was an illustration of the fact that outward acts of sin proceed from the innermost part of a person's being.

Most of us would be shocked to admit thoughts of hatred and murder in our hearts. Yet, we will see that possibility as we identify with another person of "like passions," Cain. How then does hatred arise and in some cases become murder? We will travel into some of the darker depths of the human mind as we see possibilities of murder in each of our lives.

The Birth of Hatred

Each one of us has murderous thoughts at times. Novels such as Golding's *Lord of the Flies* and Conrad's

Heart of Darkness are an ever present reminder that this lethal member of the "seven deadly sins" is lurking in the background of our lives. The seeds of hatred are sometimes found in the hearts of people with great potential.

Hate Kills Potential

Eve was so excited the day Cain was born. She exclaimed, "With the help of the Lord I have brought forth a man," (Genesis 4:1).

Could it have been an expectation that Cain was the promised Messiah, the one to bruise the head of the serpent? The impact of such an expectation must have been with Cain through all his years of development from infancy to adulthood. Were his mother's hopes too high for the boy Cain? We don't know the answer to this question, but we would not be stretching the point to say that Cain fell far short of his potential.

At times people fall from their potential when the seeds of murder find fruitful soil in their hearts. How can we forget the Jonestown massacre? We do forget, though, that Jim Jones was a respected member of the San Francisco community. He was commended on more than one occasion for his social action on behalf of the poor and destitute. How can the mighty fall so quickly?

The Innermost Source of Hatred

There is no doubt that hate is one of the more destructive human passions. It does not just come upon us like a fever. The Devil does not make us hate. The Bible places the responsibility for the acting out of hate squarely in our laps. The apostle James talks of the history of evil human desire when he writes:

> Each one is tempted when, by his own evil desire, he is dragged away and enticed. Then, after desire has conceived, it gives birth to sin; and sin, when it is full-grown, gives birth to death.
>
> (James 1:14–15)

It is unlikely that Cain was born with hate in his heart. Over a period of years a growing jealousy built up in his mind as he watched his brother's righteous life. When we give ourselves over to the first thoughts of hatred, we conceive and then give birth to a deadly sin. Jesus holds us responsible for our inner thought life and the words used to express our unconscious sentiments. He warned that anyone who speaks to his brother with contempt and calls him a fool is in danger of punishment. (Matthew 5:22)

As a psychologist I work with family violence situations on a number of occasions. Every instance of violence begins with a sequence of inner thoughts in the mind of the spouse or child beater. Take the example of the man who says to himself, "The stupid woman, there she goes again with her nagging demands." His body tenses up, he thinks hateful thoughts, and then resorts to solving the problem through the use of violence. What he says in his mind has a direct bearing on the subsequent behavior. He illustrates the saying of Jesus that "As a man thinketh in his heart, so is he." We behave the way we think. What then were the innermost thoughts in Cain's heart?

An Arrogant Spirit Begets Hatred

Where the hatred started we do not know. We do
know that the life event that brought it to the surface
was an offering brought to the Lord. (Genesis 4:2–5)
There is some debate among Old Testament scholars as
to why the Lord was not pleased with Cain's offering.
Some say that Cain was disobedient in that he did not
bring a "blood" sacrifice. That would be true if the worship event had been related to the sin sacrifice. However
the more likely explanation is that Cain was somewhat
arrogant in the worship of the Lord. The issue was not
the material content of the offering but the Lord's evalu-
ation of the motivation of the heart. Cain got the message. The Lord was not pleased with his offering (v. 5).
He came to Cain and confronted him on the anger
shown clearly on his face (v. 6). Cain envied his brother's
good standing with the Lord. The envy turned to hate.
We now note the challenge of the Lord to Cain and see
that it still applies to us today.

We Are Responsible for Our Passions

The Lord challenged Cain to take care of the hate in
his heart before it led to a greater disaster (v. 7). He gave
him an opportunity to repent. Cain was warned that his
inner attitude of hate and envy was like a wild beast
waiting at the door to devour him. He was told that he
should master this inner festering passion. Here was a
direct appeal to his sense of personal responsibility. His
brooding over his brother's acceptance with the Lord
was not helpful and could lead to other sinful acts. Again

we see that short distance between an inner emotion and an outward act. The Lord does not make the inner/outer distinction. Note the apostle John's words, "Anyone who hates his brother is a murderer," (1 John 3:15). Cain let his passions have free reign and as a result actually murdered his brother. The lesson is that we need to deal with our secret destructive passions before they destroy others as well.

The Consequences of Hatred

Hatred nursed in our inner being is condemned by God and destructive to our own well-being. However, hatred expressed in outward acts of criticism, gossip, and sometimes murder also has terrible personal and social consequences. Now most of us will never commit actual acts of murder but we will still have hatred towards another person. We will now examine how such hatred impacts other people.

Social Responsibility

The question of the Lord to Cain—"Where is your brother?"—indicates that people are not islands unto themselves in the expression of hatred. Any act of aggression on our part has a ripple effect on humankind. Take for instance an act of family violence. Not only is the victim harmed but other members of the family and community are harmed as well. Abused children sometimes become abusing parents. Sexually abused children sometimes become teenage runaways and prostitutes. We cannot escape the responsibility for our acts of personal and domestic violence. We can say the same for acts of international violence. The Lord challenges nations like the U.S.A. with "Where is your brother?" We cannot violate other nations such as Viet Nam without suffering the consequences of incidents like the "boat people." The blood of the oppressed cries out to the Lord. We are obliged to make amends for all our acts of violence. What then will our response be? Certainly it should not be like that of Cain.

Personal Denial

The callous response of Cain was "Am I my brother's keeper?" Such a crass denial of personal responsibility is found in a variety of social situations. Take for example the Watergate conspirators who repeatedly credited their acts as mere obedience to authorities. The guards in the Polish concentration camps also sought to avoid the responsibility of killing millions of Jewish people. Not only did Cain deny personal responsibility for his murderous act but he was plain sassy to God. His literal words were "Shall I shepherd the shepherd?" Sometimes the degree of our belligerence in response to an accusation is a direct measure of our responsibility. The Lord does not let us off the hook easily.

After David the king had murdered a citizen of the land and tried to cover it up, God sent a prophet, Nathan, to David to say, "Thou art the man." He sends the Holy Spirit to "convict us of sin, righteousness, and judgement." David ultimately responded with a prayer of confession that is recorded in Psalm 51. Cain, however, had to eat of the fruits of his unrepentant heart.

Personal Consequences

To some extent we all live with the consequences of our misdeeds. In Genesis 4:12, Cain was told that there would be both vocational as well as personal ramifications for the death of his brother. The scars of the past still have the ability to remind us of our hurt. Like Cain, we say "My punishment is more than I can bear." In the midst of such cries of remorse we need to remember that the Lord is still merciful and forgiving.

The mark of Cain (v. 15) was an act of *mercy* from God rather than a judgement. I hear some terrible stories of past misdeeds in my consultations with my patients. Sometimes they are directly responsible for the sins of the past. After they have done all that they can to make restitution with the victims of their hatred they still live with the remorse. One of the most powerful passages of Scripture that I leave with them is from the prophet Joel, "I will repay you for the years the locusts have eaten," (Joel 2:25).

The nation had come under the judgement of God for her waywardness. Heathen nations had been used on a number of occasions like locusts that devour a crop. Little life is left in the wake of a locust plague. The promise was that new shoots would emerge in time and that there would be another harvest. Time and again people testify to the mercy of God that restores them to hope and usefulness again. The mercy of God would let Cain have his harvest time again.

A Personal Life Response

To what extent has hatred towards others produced hurt in your life? Consider God's mercy to Cain and some of the great promises of forgiveness in Scripture such as Micah 7:18.

Applying the Truth

- To what extent has sibling rivalry been a motivating force in your life?
- To what degree do you nurse hatred towards another person?
- To what extent are you evading the responsibility for your strong passion of hatred?
- In what areas are we as a nation our "brother's keeper" in relationship to other nations?

Gratitude: More Than a Thank-You Card

What Do You Think?

In this life people generally get what they deserve.	Yes	No	Maybe
The experience of forgiveness and the expression of gratitude go hand in hand.	Yes	No	Maybe
Strong emotions and clear thought do not go together in the worship of God.	Yes	No	Maybe

Gratitude: More Than a Thank-You Card

When it comes to gratitude some people don't even get as far as sending a thank-you card. Most of us believe that when good things come our way we are getting our just deserts. On the other hand, when ill fortune comes it is a result of bad luck or the other person's fault.

Let us consider Luke 7:36–50. The story before us is of a woman who did not get what she deserved, at least as far as Simon the Pharisee was concerned. To him she was an outcast of society, a prostitute, and the sort of person he avoided like the plague lest he become ceremonially unclean for temple worship and duty. Jesus accepted her as a person and forgave her sins. Simon had a lot to learn about forgiveness and gratitude.

Luke does not tell us the woman's name. All we know is that she was a prostitute and grateful to Jesus for the provision of forgiveness and acceptance. Are you able to identify with her expression of gratitude? Do you feel any enthusiasm in the worship of Jesus for the forgiveness of your sin? What difference does his acceptance of your person make to your life? The woman in Luke 7 has a lot to teach us about gratitude and its expression.

Reasons for Gratitude

We usually gravitate towards our own "in crowd" and stay away from actual or perceived rejection. Not so with this woman. She went straight into the hornet's nest in Simon's house. The way Jesus dealt with her presents a stark contrast to the attitude of Simon. The contrast highlights one reason why she came to express gratitude. Jesus accepted her as a person.

The Acceptance of Her Person

We all like to put our best foot forward when we meet new people. Somehow we want their first impression of us to count towards a good relationship in the future. Sometimes we don't go beyond superficiality in relationships because of a fear of rejection. It is quite common for people to come to my office for their first session of psychotherapy and not tell me the worst about themselves. One of the chief reasons people return for the second session is that they felt accepted as persons in the initial encounter.

The woman in Luke 7 could walk into a foreign environment because of the acceptance that she felt from Jesus. A person with her history would never enter a gathering of religious persons like the Pharisees. It was the presence of Jesus that attracted her to the gathering. Apparently there had been a previous interaction between her and the Master. Perhaps she had been a part of a crowd that heard him preach on forgiveness. She was confident on the basis of her past association with him that he would accept her. She showed courage. It is quite amazing how unconditional acceptance from another gives us the confidence to act with courage even in the most adverse circumstances. We now move to a dimension of acceptance unique to the Christian faith, forgiveness of sin.

The Forgiveness of Her Sin

George Bernard Shaw is reputed to have criticized forgiveness as "a beggar's refuge." On the contrary, it is the only refuge sinners have before a holy God. Of all the religions of the world, Christianity is the only one that presents a deity that fully and freely forgives sin. It is because of the grace expressed in Jesus that we stand before God with a clean slate.

Never in this woman's life had she experienced such a profound acceptance from another person. He assured her that her sins were forgiven. In verse 47 Jesus says, "I tell you, her many sins have been forgiven—for she loved much. But he who has been forgiven little loves little."

The greater the sense of our sinfulness, the greater the gratitude when we experience God's forgiveness. As a psychologist, I have seen that the forgiveness of God is the greatest therapeutic agent in the world. How a person can transcend the hurts and injustices of the past without forgiveness is beyond me.

I have vivid memories of Alice, an ex-prostitute, who was in counselling for depression. As a child she had suffered from many episodes of sexual abuse by her father. It was only in her thirties that she began to recall the details of the incest. All her life she had been afraid of men, rejection, and true intimacy. She went through the painful process of remembering the abuse. She then struggled with the issue of whether she should forgive her father. An even bigger battle was whether she should forgive herself for the years of prostitution. Slowly and painfully she found forgiveness in the Lord. I continually reassured her that she was a forgiven person in Christ. I took seriously the fact that I had the authority, as do all believers, to announce to her the forgiveness of her sin.

Gradually her depression lifted and she became a productive person for the first time in her life. Her sense of gratitude towards the Lord was a constant theme in her discourse with others.

The Expression of Gratitude

Gratitude is not a private experience. It finds its expression in concrete and sometimes costly responses. A thank-you card is sometimes the least that we can do to express our gratitude. The woman in Luke 7 expressed her gratitude with a passion that serves as a lesson for us all. She was unashamed and uninhibited in her grateful response to the Master. Not only did she come into the house of Simon the Pharisee, but she interrupted the feast with her intense and outward show of gratitude. She touched Jesus, which was something that a woman would never do to a rabbi. She also undid her hair in public, another scandalous act for her time and culture.

For all these acts she had to overcome a natural human inclination to be inhibited by the opinion of others.

One Sunday at a morning worship service, our pastor encouraged us to raise our hands while we sang praises to our Lord. In my noncharismatic church tradition, such an act of worship seemed awfully strange. Some of the congregation spontaneously adopted this form of worship. My arms seemed stuck to my sides. My chief concern was what would people think of me if I raised my hands in worship. It only took me a few minutes to overcome this ridiculous concern with the opinions of people.

The Focus on Jesus

In recent months I have been introduced to the discipline of contemplative prayer. My teacher, the books I read on the subject, and the discipline itself help me focus on one thing at a time. I find a quiet and restful place in my home. I make sure there are no distractions, like children or the telephone. First, I relax myself through a focus on my breathing. I then shut distracting thoughts out of my mind. The next step is to imagine myself walking in a peaceful place with Jesus. I do not speak to him but just enjoy his presence. I work on becoming totally involved in the experience of his person. At times I have to fight off distracting thoughts. It is a very difficult process because I was taught that prayer involved much talk on my part. I have great admiration for my Roman Catholic brothers and sisters schooled in the practice of contemplative prayer. I identify with the woman who shut out the distractions of Simon's feast and focused entirely on Jesus. Her mind could have been distracted by thoughts of how others would respond to her behavior. Yet, her grateful interaction with the Master was so intense that she became "lost in wonder, love, and praise." Can we say the same of our acts of praise to God?

Gratitude Is Costly and Specific

It is not enough to just say "I feel grateful." Faith without works is dead. It cost the woman a lot to express her gratitude. She poured expensive ointment on the Master. Even the container was made of alabaster, a fine translucent stone used for decorative pieces, and very costly. The bigger cost however was her willingness to ignore the social stigma of her act and worship Jesus. If we could have debriefed her after the event, she probably would have denied that it involved sacrifice on her part. That is typical of persons who give of themselves for Christ and the world. An observer thinks that they are making a great sacrifice, but they feel that their act is the expression of the joy of their heart.

Her act of gratitude was also specific in its expression. It was not a vague sentimentality expressed in a "Oh, how I love him." She gave of herself and her substance. Each one of us has unique ways to give of our person to the Lord. We give, not out of duty or guilt, but out of gratitude.

Expressed With Strong Emotion

Our gratitude can be expressed with strong feelings. King David danced before the Lord. The apostle John was lost in adoration for the Lord in his apocalyptic vision. Isaiah responded in awe to the vision of the Lord by saying "Woe to me." We sometimes avoid the expression of strong passion in the worship of the Lord. We keep things "decent and in order" at the expense of emotion. Church services tend to be an exercise of our rationality more than the expression of our whole person.

The woman worshipped her Lord with strong emotion. She smothered him with kisses. She wept profusely. In worshipful abandon she untied her hair and dried her tears from his feet. Such an act of worship in many churches today would cause the person to be expelled from the building by the ushers. The Lord wants to be worshipped in Spirit and in truth. Sometimes the Spirit blows where he wills and calls us to transcend the bounds of formality.

The Results of Gratitude

It is impossible to express strong emotion in the worship of the Lord without a response from others and the Lord. A grateful person is a pain in the neck for certain people. Have you ever been in the company of a group of people in the midst of a "pity party"? The focus of the discussion is on the awful state of affairs in their world. You interject a word of praise to the discussion. The silence is icy as they regard you with disdain. Their attitude is "how dare this person change the climate of our discussion from negative to positive." Gratitude has very definite results.

A Rebuke to the Ungrateful

Jesus exposed Simon the Pharisee as an ungrateful person. Simon sensed little need for forgiveness. He was downright rude in his attitude to Jesus. He did not even extend the common courtesies of the day to his guest. So, Jesus told him a parable of a person who forgave two debtors. One owed him a large sum of money, the other a smaller amount. He forgave both of the debts. The pointed question to Simon was "Which one would be more grateful?" Simon's response was in line with the obvious application of the story, "The one he forgave the most." We are not told what happened to Simon. The most productive response to such a rebuke from the Lord is that people like Simon should change their minds. The opposite is often true. People harden their hearts in the face of acceptance and forgiveness.

I stand amazed at how often we reject the goodness of God. Maybe we are too preoccupied with our unworthiness. Some of us have experienced such massive doses of rejection in our past that we find it very difficult to trust anybody, including God. As a result, God is seen as an extension of the ones who rejected us. The hurts of the past need to be healed before we can learn to trust God for the first time. The process of healing involves an honest admission of the depth of our hurt. We then need to forgive the persons who have brought the pain of rejection to our lives.

Another reason some can't express gratitude to God is that they, like Simon, are caught up in a religion of legalism. Such a faith seeks to earn the favor of God through the performance of good works. Modern Pharisees are exhausted by a demanding program of religious activity, compulsive attention to "correct" behavior, and a judgmental attitude towards persons outside of the system. The message of the Lord to them is, "For I desire mercy, not sacrifice, and acknowledgment of God rather than burnt offerings," (Hosea 6:6).

The experience of mercy is one of accepting the grace of the Lord. We cannot earn his favor. It is a free gift in Christ. We are also to show this mercy towards others in a life of the active pursuit of justice. It is only after such an experience of God's acceptance that we can be freed from the bonds of legalism.

Peace With Herself and God

After Jesus had assured the woman that her sins were forgiven, He encouraged her with a common benediction of the day, "Go in peace." It is only after we have experienced such acceptance in Jesus that we can know true peace in our hearts.

The feeling that "it is well with my soul" is one of the greatest confidence-building truths from the Bible. The apostle Paul captures this truth in Romans 5:1, "Therefore, since we have been justified through faith, we have peace with God through our Lord Jesus Christ."

All her life this woman had been used, rejected, and considered an outcast. Because of the acceptance given by Jesus, she could at last experience peace within herself. The benediction "Go in peace" was the legacy of her encounter with the acceptance and forgiveness of Christ. A life changing truth indeed.

A Personal Life Response

To what degree does the forgiveness of your sin generate feelings and acts of gratitude in your life?

Applying the Truth

- When last did you really feel accepted as a person?
- To what degree and on what grounds can we forgive ourselves and others?
- Could you walk into a cool or hostile environment and still feel good about yourself?
- Make a list of the ways you can express your gratitude to God and others.
- Discuss the ways that you can express gratitude for sins forgiven.
- Why is it imperative that we forgive others?

The Prophet Who Sang
the Blues

What Do You Think?

All a depressed person needs is to trust God and pray more.	Yes	No	Maybe
The source of depression is mostly physical.	Yes	No	Maybe
Illogical thoughts and the "blues" go hand in hand.	Yes	No	Maybe
There are different degrees and types of depression.	Yes	No	Maybe

The Prophet Who Sang
the Blues

As twentieth century people, you and I live in a world that has a bad case of the "blues." We speak of the economy as being depressed—or, at least, unstable. Popular music decries the loss of love, the loss of purpose, the loss of personhood. Our society suffers from a negative view of the person, the future, and the world in general. All of these attitudes and fears, when carried to the extreme, are characteristic components of depression.

Two words that capture the essence of depression are loss and helplessness. Depressed people have lost their health, love, jobs, esteem, and the ability to bounce back from adversity. They have reached the point where, to one degree or another, they are helpless spiritually, emotionally and physically.

Depression is a common part of human experience. Each of us has or will be depressed some time in our lives. As we walk through Elijah the prophet's experience of the "blues" in 1 Kings 19, we will be better equipped both to understand, as well as manage, our own depression.

The Characteristics of Depression

Elijah found himself under pressure. Many demands had fallen on the shoulders of the veteran prophet within a short span of time. In chapter 18 alone, Elijah had confrontations with King Ahab himself, 850 pagan prophets (over half of whom he eventually killed in one afternoon), and the cruel queen Jezebel. At the end of the chapter he even outran the king in his chariot. He had just completed the equivalent of an "iron-man" marathon. It is no wonder that he was exhausted and succumbed to the thoughts and feelings of depression.

Yet it is important to note that the stresses of the day, even though severe, cannot be blamed for the onset of his depression. If we study Elijah's situation a bit closer, several causes for his bout with the "blues" will begin to appear.

A Twisted Interpretation

The way we interpret our experiences often determines whether or not we become depressed. Persons who are depressed generally perceive themselves as helpless and as losers. Such self-evaluation, however, does not usually harmonize with all the facts. In 1 Kings 18, we see Elijah in the midst of success and victory in his encounter with the prophets of Baal. Yet within a short time, he is overcome with his own defeatism: "Take my life; I am no better than my ancestors,"(v. 4), and "I am the only one left." (v. 10). These words were in response to Jezebel's threat on his life. In a fit of rage she had promised to kill him within twenty-four hours of his massacre of the prophets of Baal. But it was not Jezebel's threat which caused Elijah's depression. Rather, it was his pessimistic interpretation of the threat. First, a negative dialog took place. Then came the words of panic and despair. Elijah did not flee into the wilderness without first thinking "Jezebel intends to kill me and I am helpless in the face of such a threat." He did not intend to resign from his prophetic ministry without a preceding chain of thought: "I am the only one left and now they are trying to kill me too." The basis for his despair was a negative view of himself, the world, the past and the future.

Elijah could have learned from the wisdom of the ancient philosopher Epictetus. He wrote, "Men are not disturbed by things but by the view which they take of them." The Bible, too, emphasizes the impact of inner thoughts on outward behavior in Proverbs 23:7, "As a man thinketh in his heart so is he." Our thought life has an impact on our action, but so does our physical state.

A Tired Body

The prophet was exhausted. Depression can also be the result of prolonged demands on the human body. Such stress, if mismanaged, can help lower our defenses and increase the likelihood of personal breakdown. Researchers have identified two kinds of stress: eustress and distress. The prefix *eu* means good. It is important to realize that happy times can be stressful. A graduation, marriage, successful performance of a task, or even a promotion are events that provide eustress. Distress is even more draining. Negative demands fall into two main categories: life events and daily hassels. Demanding life events are long term. They include the death of a loved one, worries about debt and a move to a new environment. Daily hassels include freeway traffic, lost keys, and worries about weight. Both types of stress have the ability to drain our productive energies and push us to the point of depression.

Elijah succumbed to the cumulative effects of stress and became depressed. His physical system was strained to the point of breaking. His nervous system remained on the red alert for too long. Adrenalin pumped through his body for hours without respite. His heart and lungs had to work overtime to keep him going. It is a known fact that if this physiological state continues unabated, exhaustion soon sets in. Signs of such exhaustion in our lives include slowness of movement; disruption of fine motor movement, like the inability to thread a needle or play a guitar; excessive sleep; and general physical lethargy.

Consider the demands Elijah placed on his body over the period of a few short days. His battle on Mount Carmel had led to a great victory for God but had drained the prophet. Following this incredible expenditure of energy, he actually outran the king's chariot from Carmel to Jezreel. He then had to run for his life from Queen Jezebel. All these demands were a prelude to the scene in the desert. There, he sat under the meager shade of the broom tree, and cried out to God, "I have had enough, Lord, take my life." With these words he fell into an exhausted sleep.

Mental Exhaustion

The picture of the prophet in the desert is also one of a person under severe mental strain. Tired minds go with tired bodies. When he sat down under the broom tree, he was no longer able to think logically and clearly. Statements like "let me die" and "I am no better than my ancestors" are hardly models of lucid thought. This is not to say that Elijah was a weakling. Even the strongest person, after hours of intense pressure, sometimes breaks down wimpering before God and others. Like the poet William Cowper, many of us have gone before the Lord in a state of deep mental discouragement, and said, "Where is the blessedness I knew, when first I saw the Lord?"

The question arises, Were Elijah's illogical thoughts the cause or the result of his depression? An exhausted person is often an irrational person. Most depressed people find it difficult to concentrate. They find it difficult to pray. God seems light years away. They cry out for relief from their situation. They illogically blame outward situations as the cause of their negative emotions.

A Tendency to Blame Circumstances

So often we blame our circumstances for our trials and blues. Like Elijah, we become mentally paralyzed and lash out at our situation. In Elijah's case, the blazing fire of Carmel had been reduced to the cold grey ashes of inactivity. In his mind, he interpreted Jezebel's threat as meaning that everyone hated him and wished him dead. He perceived his ministry as being a waste of time, just

like the ministries of all the prophets and saints before
him. (1 Kings 19:10) The situation indeed looked bleak.

And yet it was his interpretation of the situation
which was bleak. For contrast, it is important to look at
the example of Jesus in a similar situation. The Bible
narrative records, "Then all the disciples deserted him
and fled," (Matthew 26:56). The loss of supportive
friends could have been prime occasion for depression,
especially when pressed to the limits as our Lord was in
the twenty-four hours before his death. Yet, we see Jesus
rising above the circumstances. He expresses confidence
in the Father who could press twelve legions of angels
into service on behalf of his Son if he willed.

Any person who stands for God against popular opinion and unjust causes will at times be alone. The very
fact that we are part of the bundle of life means that we
will suffer loss. Yet, it is how we interpret our circumstances that often decides the depth of our despair or the
extent of our joy. The same person who complained that
the Israelites had, "rejected your covenant, broken down
your altars, and put your prophets to death with the
sword," had called down fire from heaven on the altar at
Mount Carmel and had soundly defeated the prophets of
Baal on the previous day.

A Loss of Meaning

A depressed person has a negative and anxious view
of the future. Hopelessness is evident on every front.
Twice God asked Elijah, "What are you doing here?"
And he responded how his ministry had been in vain,
and his future was hopeless. He, like Christian in *Pil-*

grim's Progress, was trapped in the slough of despond. He could not see the stepping stones of hope.

Like the brooding prophet, the depressed person also loses a sense of the meaning of the past. Elijah discounted not only his own ministry, but also the ministry of previous prophets. Unlike the apostle Paul, who in the face of impending death evaluated his life and stated he had fought a good fight and run a winning race, Elijah viewed his past as valueless. Like Elijah, when it happens in our lives, all the moments that we have built in the strength of the Lord are destroyed by our negative assessment of ourselves and the future. When the correct perspective of the past is lost, the meaning of our life and future is covered by the black cloud of depression.

Physical Causes

Unlike the example of Elijah, there are occasions when we may experience a negative change in mood for no apparent reason. At times such as these, it may be important to get medical help. Certain physical diseases have depression as their outward manifestation. Sometimes, also, prescribed and non-prescribed drugs result in mood changes. In other cases, a prolonged period of severe stress leads the person into depression. Elijah is a prime example of a person who, at a time of physical exhaustion, succumbed to feelings of depression. We don't know whether he had been through a similar experience before, but his response to the experience shows poor coping skills. I often encounter people in my practice who are completely surprised by their depression. I hear responses like "This can't be happening to me, I am usually such an optimistic person." Generally, in those cases, there is some physical basis for the depression. Rest, corrective diet, exercise, and medication are part of the solution.

The Management of Depression

My experience as a Christian psychologist, the research literature on depression, and my personal experience with bouts of the blues lead me to conclude that many factors are involved in the healing of depression. There are no easy answers. The most important factor, however, is found in accurate diagnosis. If the cause is mainly physical, a course of anti-depressive medication alleviates the problem. If the person's helplessness is sustained by irrational thoughts, a re-education of the mind may be indicated. There are many paths towards a cure. Let's return to 1 Kings 19 and see how the Lord mercifully treated Elijah, in order for us to get a biblical perspective on the healing of depressed persons.

Meeting Physical Needs

God's first step in treating his depressed person was very practical. He let him sleep. Then he sent his angel on two occasions with food and water (1 Kings 19:5–8). How encouraging it is that the Lord did not hammer the prophet with rebuke or flood his mind with moralistic exhortations about his lack of trust in the sovereignty of

God. Rather, He prepared the man to hear his voice by first meeting his physical needs.

In the midst of depression, time out to eat and sleep is essential. Busy parents of small children need time out. Preachers need their day off. Business executives need opportunities to leave their work behind them. Sometimes these "away" times should involve physical activity to give the person with a sedentary job a change of pace. We all need islands of tranquility in our lives. These pauses in the rapid pace of life should be made on a daily basis and not just during our annual vacation. Someone has wisely stated that we can't have music without pauses between the notes. In the same way, we cannot live productive lives without times of rest. We need to heed bodily signals like headaches, colitis, muscle tension, and bouts of depression.

Listening for God's Voice

After God had met the prophet's physical needs, Elijah was prepared to hear his voice—to gain God's perspective on his life situation. That comforting voice came to the prophet in two ways.

The Still Small Voice. Following Elijah's time of resting out in the wilderness, he traveled forty days until he came to Horeb, the mountain of God. Here he experienced the unleashing of tremendous natural forces in wind, earthquake, and fire, and yet the voice of God was not present in any of these. Instead, God came to the prophet in the whisper of soft, intelligible words. The lesson for the weary prophet, fresh from the stern and dramatic challenge of Mount Carmel, was that the victories of life often come in the humble and unobtrusive. Gentle love is often stronger than force, compassionate persuasion mightier than compulsion.

The best way to smash a rock is not always with a sledge hammer. A smaller tool is often quite sufficient. First, find the fault line in the rock. Then tap away at its point of weakness. After a while, a relatively small tool can break apart a large boulder. In a similar manner, a discouraged person needs to hear the still small voice of encouragement.

In an age of sensationalism with its moon landings, banner headlines, super churches, and dynamic personalities, we run to the promise of the bright and flashy in search of miracle cures for our inner hurts. Yet God still chooses to speak in a still small voice. Depressed persons generally have a short attention span, a narrow range of receptivity, and a short emotional fuse. In this condition they need empathy—a few appropriate and sensitive words not a blast of censure or advice. Wisdom can come in small packages.

The Challenging Voice. God spoke softly to Elijah, but he also disputed the prophet's irrational and confused thinking. Then he sent him back to work. The prophet, in his weakened state, experienced a loss of meaning. The Lord ministered to this vacuum of disillusionment.

Each of us suffers loss in life. We may lose a close friend or family member, a prized possession or job. When loss occurs our first tendency is to interpret it wrongly, telling ourselves, for instance, "I will never have a friend like that again. It took me such a long time to develop such a meaningful relationship." Our emotions become entangled in the web of self-destructive thinking. We cease sleeping at night as we toss restlessly in an attempt to resolve our dilemma of meaning. The Lord speaks in a soft, challenging voice saying "What are you doing here?"

Recently I went through a mild mid-life crisis where I struggled with the meaning of my life. I looked at all my achievements and my response to them was "So what, there must be more to life than this!" I battled with depression even though I sensed the presence and acceptance of God in my life. A friend of mine taught me some of the principles of contemplative prayer. During one of these periods, the still small voice of the Lord spoke to me. In effect, the Lord told me that my value as a person consisted in my being and not so much in my doing. I had a personal value to God far beyond my performance. The meaning of my life was to be found in the fact that I was God's child, fashioned in his image. There was nothing that I could do to earn God's acceptance. I was already accepted in Christ. As the message from the Lord penetrated my fog of confusion, the depression lifted.

Irrational beliefs bring with them life-crippling consequences. For each disabling thought that floods our minds, there is a biblical truth that comes as the soft, intelligible, and clearly focused answer. As Christians, we do not deny the reality of the losses in our lives. Death, departures, desertions, and declining abilities are facts in our existence. Yet, how we interpret these is another matter. We can have power over our losses to the degree that we evaluate them biblically and rationally.

A Personal Life Response

Examine some of Elijah's irrational internal dialog which contributed to his depression. Then consider God's answer which challenged each faulty perception, as laid out in the chart below:

Problem	Elijah	God
Isolation	"I am alone" (v. 10).	"Seven thousand faithful remain" (v. 18).
Failure	"My work is useless and I have failed (v. 10).	"You still have work to do" (v. 15).
Insecurity	"I am no better than my fathers" (v. 4).	"My work goes on despite difficulties" (v. 17).
Fear	"My enemies are out to kill me" (v. 10).	"I will take care of the enemy" (v. 17)
Meaning	"I want to die" (v. 4).	"Get back to work" (v. 15).

Are there areas of irrational thinking which have caused you to wrongly interpret your life circumstances as threatening? Can you identify them? What does the still small voice of the Lord say to you to calm and correct your thinking?

Are you a depressed person? If you can answer affirmatively to most of the following questions, you are more than likely suffering from depression.

- Have your interest in life and your ability to enjoy it diminished markedly?
- Has your weight or appetite increased or decreased?
- Are you sleeping too much or too little?
- Is your energy level low, and do you tire easily?
- Are your bodily movements agitated or very slow?
- Are you filled with self-reproach and guilt?
- Has your ability to think and concentrate decreased?
- Do you have recurring thoughts of death or suicide?
- Have most of the above continued for more than two weeks?

Applying the Truth

- When was the last time you took time out from your daily routine, through vacation, recreation, or prayer and meditation? When can you do it again? How can you make "time out" a more consistent and regular priority?
- Evaluate what you say to yourself in terms of:
  A negative view of yourself, circumstances, and the future.
  Who you blame for your depression.
- Look for a group of people in your community who can nurture you in a tender, yet tough, manner.
- Get a thorough medical check-up.
- Find a skilled Christian therapist who will walk with you to new wholeness.

- Evaluate the meaningfulness of your life from a practical, scriptural perspective. What are your spiritual gifts? Where can you best be investing your life? Consult your pastor and get back into the service of God's family.

How to Help a Depressed Person

In cases of extended episodes of depression, family members and friends tend to become impatient with the person with the blues. Some Christians become judgemental that the depressed person has not "been delivered," "trusted the Lord," or "snapped out of it." Such attitudes do not show sensitivity and knowledge of the causes and cure of depression. Many of our easy prescriptions do not help. If we follow some of the procedures below, we may prove to be more helpful.

- One person cannot provide total support for another in distress. Nurture yourself and find other helpers.
- Keep silent and help in practical ways, like taking the depressed person for walks or to events that will prove to be pleasurable for him or her.
- Don't blame yourself for the person's depression.
- Take suicide threats seriously, especially if there have been previous attempts.
- Listen to the person and let him or her hear non-judgemental prayers.
- Read all you can about the causes and cure for depression.

Green With Envy

It is natural and healthy for persons to compare themselves with each other.	Yes	No	Maybe
God promises that life on earth will be fair sooner or later.	Yes	No	Maybe
One of the major causes of bitterness in a person is comparisons with others.	Yes	No	Maybe

Green With Envy

We have all had fantasies about the "happy" rich, the "lucky" celebrity, the "noble" poor, and the "good old" days. They can arouse passionate feelings of longing in the person who is passing through difficult times. One of the feelings likely to be aroused is that of envy. The writer of Psalm 73 went through the passion of envy just like we do. He writes, "I envied the arrogant."

I remember once during graduate school walking along the immaculately kept pier at a beach city in California, surveying with great envy the ocean-going yachts. The houses on the shore matched the opulence seen in the boats. Surely these people must be happier than I am, I thought. But is such a notion fact or myth? We all know that riches do not in themselves sentence a person to a life of misery or great happiness. Financially, the owners of the boats were the "haves." I was a "have not." Compared to my feelings of unmet physical need, surely these folks, were happier than I was. The irony of the situation is that compared to ninety percent of the rest of the world, my possessions constitute me as a "have." Somehow envy twists our thinking into unreality.

The Conflict: Verses 1–14

The writer of Psalm 73 must have had an experience similar to mine the day I surveyed the wealthy from the pier. At any rate, he goes into great detail describing the conflict that he feels. His dominant theme, in the first fourteen verses of the psalm is "poor me," versus "lucky them." Evidently his circumstances were pressing. It appears that they included emotional struggles, physical ill-health, and financial burdens. Added to these, his greatest struggle related to his misperception of the lot of the rich who were ungodly. He states, "They have no struggles, their bodies are healthy and strong. They are free from the burdens common to man; they are not plagued by human ills."

His intense conflict was complicated by a series of mental errors that grew out of his wrong comparison of himself with the so-called prosperous wicked persons he saw all around him. Some of these errors are the ones that twentieth-century people are likely to make as well. Let us look at some of the common mistakes in reasoning made by the psalmist.

The Happy Celebrity

We live in a day when celebrities are glorified by the media, worshipped by the world's discontented, and given a status just short of secular sainthood. The covert message to all of us is that unless we are celebrities, we are of little significance. Unfortunately, this point of view infects the Christian, as well as the secular, world. Some international evangelists, Christian television talk-show hosts, pastors of superchurches, and Christian publishing houses feature converted celebrities as a part of the gospel presentation. Even in the realm of Christian higher education, graduate schools and colleges play the "publish or perish" game with their faculty and students. The focus is on the praise of people rather than the approval of God. Today the apostle Paul would probably not be a featured guest on some of the Christian talk-shows. He was a poor public speaker, and certainly was not the blond, blue-eyed All-American football player guaranteed to draw a crowd. Apparently this climate is one source of the happy celebrity myth.

The problem with celebrity worship is one of self-esteem and denial of mortality. We boost our sagging egos with the thought that we know some famous person. I remember with some amusement an incident from my seminary years. One of the visiting speakers tried to impress us with how many times he "sat on the platform," a place of prestige, at Billy Graham rallies. We also try to link ourselves with celebrities to deal with our fear of death. Somehow, through association with such people, we insure a place for ourselves in time and eternity. Their contribution to life serves to reinforce our contribution to life. In our self-hate we minimize the divine stamp on our nature which has been redeemed by Christ. We bring glory to God and to ourselves by being ourselves and not other people. A oak tree brings glory to God by being an oak tree, not a redwood tree. Envy of another person is a way of putting oneself down and insuring personal misery. If we need to "name drop" for a sense of significance, we do well to identify ourselves as children of the King of Kings.

High Frequency "Poor Talk"

The more we talk and complain about our woeful lot in life, the more dissatisfied with it we become. In times of great trial we tend to become very sorry for ourselves. We indulge in "pity parties" where we proclaim to ourselves and the world our desperate plight. Such constant rehearsal of misery causes us to lose a healthy perspective on God's involvement in our lives. There is a place for the sharing of the hurts of life. We are encouraged to share each other's burdens. However, we come to a point of diminishing returns in sharing problems when we no longer find hope through our faith in the Lord. We also find that "poor me" talk tends to reinforce our misery. It is like attempting to douse hot coals with gasoline. The act only causes the fire to flare up once again. We need to take note of the negative statements that recur with high frequency in our lives. If we constantly complain and agonize about our financial position, we inflame our misery unnecessarily. If we have poor physical health, frequent "organ recitals" increase our personal distress.

We need to learn to look beyond the horizons of our personal misery to the protective power of God. Again, I am not advocating a denial of our hurts or a "Polyanna" view of life. I seek, with the apostle Paul, to find constructive thought patterns as a solution for my anxieties.

He wrote, "Finally brothers, whatever is true, whatever is noble, whatever is right, whatever is pure, whatever is lovely, whatever is admirable—if anything is excellent or praiseworthy—think about such things," (Philippians 4:8).

Godliness Does Not Pay

As a final, discouraging note, the psalmist said, "Surely in vain I have kept my heart pure." In contrast, the apostle Paul writing from prison noted that ". . . godliness with contentment is great gain," (1 Timothy 6:6).

The contrast between the two experiences is great. The disgruntled psalmist saw that his attempts at living a godly life did not result in prosperity, wealth, and success. His emotional pain was protracted and intense. "All day long I have been plagued; I have been punished every morning," (Psalm 73:14).

Yet the one inflicting pain was himself. It did not happen to him. His godliness was not in vain; he merely misinterpreted the results of his piety. Blessedness lay in another sphere. How could he have forgotten the words of David, "Blessed is he whose transgressions are forgiven, whose sins are covered," (Psalm 32:1). Fortunately, though, the discouraged writer of Psalm 73 was soon to relearn the meaning of prosperity.

The Contemplation: Verses 15–16

Verse fifteen portrays a man with a dilemma. He wanted to share his conflict with his people. Yet he felt that he couldn't broadcast his doubts. He writes, "If I had said, 'I will speak thus,' I would have betrayed this generation of your children."

There are times when a person must keep a conflict inside and refuse to verbalize it to others. I am intrigued as to why this man had to remain silent. Could it be that he was a leader, and that: 1) people didn't expect their leaders to have doubts; 2) there was a shortage of caring people with discretion within his circle of fellowship who would not make his problems public knowledge; or 3) he didn't want to mislead those whose faith was weak?

All of the above options were possible then, and remain so now. Consider the example of Rick, a young pastor who consulted me regarding a crisis in his life. He told me that the people at his church would never understand his struggle and pain. He asked me not to reveal that he had come for counselling. I assured him that my professional ethics required absolute confidentiality. Yet I was amazed at the loneliness of his struggle. Just like the psalmist, he could say, "When I tried to understand all this, it was oppressive to me ..." I encouraged Rick to share some of his struggle with a couple of the elders at his church. He did and was amazed at how supportive they were. One of them told him, "It really does me good to hear you share your struggle with us. In the first place, I like the trust you have placed in me. I also feel that you are more human to me now. I thought that you did not understand my problems because you had never been in my shoes."

There are rooms of the mind that the key of brooding will not unlock. The longer we ponder, the less objective we become. Where did the psalmist gain a perspective on the plight of the ungodly and the value of godliness?

The Sanctuary: Verses 17–28

The sanctuary represents both the place and process by which we draw near to God and his people. In James 4:8 we are exhorted to "Come near to God and he will come near to you." Without this experience of closeness, we leave ourselves open to begin playing the comparison game, with its erroneous interpretation of the "seeming prosperity" of the wicked.

God's call for us to enter the sanctuary and so gain a new perspective on life is very practical. The sanctuary is not necessarily some Gothic cathedral. It includes a wide range of possibilities like fellowship with God's people or the solitude of a mountaintop retreat.

In Community

Most of us suffer sometime from the disquieting thought that we are unique in our wretchedness. As a psychologist, I often use group therapy as a means of dealing with human suffering. My patients are usually very tentative in the sharing of their human foibles at the outset of such therapy. They are quick to discover, however, an incredible sense of relief when they hear that others suffer from similar problems. The shared experience of "being in the same boat" is often the beginning of their cure. The end of the cure is found in a new connectedness with the Lord who manifests his mercy through his agents in this world who accept us in our pain. Acceptance is not a permissive toleration of evil in the world. It is the valuing of persons despite their dark stream. The more merciful the fellowship of the sanctuary, the more likely it is that we gain God's perspective on our suffering. We do not always need others to gain this perspective. Sometimes in the solitude of nature we hear God say, "Be still and know that I am God."

In Solitude

A sanctuary is a place of shelter, refuge, and quiet. We all need to hear the divine call to "Come apart for a while and rest." Our sanctuary may be a quiet corner in the home, free from the distractions of life. It could also be an isolated beach. The important thing is that we free ourselves from the noisy clutter of life and get alone with God in silence. Too often our communion with the Lord is filled with our chatter. Prayers of petition are necessary but we also need to be still and hear the voice of the Lord. However, silent contemplation of God is not the end of the sanctuary experience. The person who makes the inward journey to the soul must make the outward journey to God's world.

In the World

We all need to learn from the saintly monk, Brother Lawrence, who practiced the presence of God in the monastery kitchen. He experienced the Lord as he washed the dishes. We can carry the inner peace of the Lord as we travel on the busy freeways of life. Our life of silent contemplation must carry us to the margins of society where people bleed for acceptance and practical help. The life of Jesus is our example. He alternated his activities between the prayers on the mountain and his ministry to physical and spiritual brokenness. A balance between contemplative prayer and compassionate ministry helps us keep a divine perspective on our world.

The psalm writer's experience in the sanctuary provided a needed perspective and corrected his negative frame of reference. "It was oppressive to me till I entered the sanctuary of God; then I understood their final destiny." He had been working himself up into a state of misery on the grounds of a misperception of a fact. The lessons of the sanctuary which he contemplated were three.

The Transitory Power of Riches

When I was in my teens, our family home burned to the ground. Many irreplaceable possessions were lost. I will always remember my mother's comment, though, as she sought to put the tragedy in perspective. "We couldn't take it with us when we died anyway," she explained. In this way my mother had rightly discerned the transitory nature of possessions. We all need a spirit of detachment towards people, possessions, and plans. We dare not peg our value as people to that of our possessions. I have heard of people who will not invite guests to a meal because their plates do not match, the paint job in the living room is not complete, or they don't have the latest clothes to wear. Some of us believe that we have committed one of the deadly sins if guests arrive suddenly and the house is untidy. We dare not let the cares and values of the world be like thorns that choke the Word of the Lord in our lives.

The suddenness of the destruction of the wicked, those who live their lives without reference to and reverence for God, is reflected in the words of the psalmist in verses 18 through 20. "Surely you place them on slippery ground; you cast them down to ruin. How suddenly are they destroyed, completely swept away by terrors!"

The accumulation of a lifetime can be swept away in a second, and yet eternity will stretch on in total emptiness for those who have disregarded God in their lifetime.

The Destructive Power of Bitter Thoughts

In verse 21, the psalmist speaks of a sour and embittered heart. Negative thinking about the nature of reality is the source of depression and embitterment. As we saw in the chapter on depression, many times a person is "singing the blues" because of a negative view of self, the world, and the future. We can really get ourselves depressed when we start playing comparison games like "the Jones' are better off than we are." The irony is that we don't really know the full story about the other person. Appearances of prosperity are very deceiving. Riches, in and of themselves, do not guarantee happiness in this world.

The experience of God in the sanctuary can restore one's perspective. The Lord has challenged me in recent days that I am being controlled by a spirit of fear in relationship to my children, economic uncertainities, and physical health. He gently invites me to hear the words,

"For God did not give us a spirit of timidity, but a spirit of power, of love and self-discipline," (2 Timothy 1:7).

Such self-mastery in the face of the fears of life is a divinely bestowed gift. It is available to all who enter the sanctuary and commune with the Lord and his people.

The Positive Power of the Sovereign Lord

In the midst of pain the psalmist discovered the power of the sovereign Lord to keep (v. 23), to guide (v. 24), to complete a job (v. 24), and to satisfy (v. 25). The path to this satisfaction, for the writer, was paved with the stones of questioning, doubt, torment, irritation and embitterment. Yet, ultimately his confused thinking that the ungoldly were enviable turned into a song of praise and righted values. Verse one sums up all that he discovered about God when he changed his focus: "Surely God is good to Israel, to those who are pure in heart." Truly it is only persons who have contemplated their sovereign Lord in the quietness of the sanctuary, in fellowship with others, and in connectedness with this needy world, who can honestly say, "God is good to me," even in the light of life's adversity.

A Personal Life Response

Have you been dissatisfied with certain aspects of your life, feeling that you deserve a better situation? Focus on the positive aspects of your situation, and on the character of God and the fact that ultimately his truth will win in the earth.

Feelings: The Limits of Expression

What Do You Think?

Men are made by God to be less emotional than women.	Yes	No	Maybe
Men generally don't want close emotional friendships, especially with other men.	Yes	No	Maybe
The feelings common to men and women are the result of cultural conditioning.	Yes	No	Maybe

Feelings: The Limits of Expression

We have all learned, at some time or another, not to trust our feelings. We have also been told that certain feelings are wrong. For some, the prohibited passion is anger. For others, especially men, the outward expression of sorrow is considered inappropriate. The result is that people hide their feelings behind a tough exterior.

The inexpressive person is also a person "of like passions." In our Western culture such limited emotional expression is often found in men. The more tender emotions like love and the expression of nurture is inhibited in the upbringing of many males. They are taught that "big boys" don't cry. Their credo is "win at all costs," even if it means hiding their feelings. The result of such overcontrol of emotions is shallowness and loneliness.

Overly expressive people, who literally "run off at the mouth" with their emotion, present another set of problems in our North American culture. People who lack impulse control and wear their feelings on their sleeve often cause problems with others. This chapter, then, is a quest for constructive channeling of emotions for those

125

who dam up their passions and those who allow their passions to rage uncontrolled.

Jesus, our example, was fully human in all his ways. He expressed a wide range of emotions and provides us with the example of a person who could channel his passions wisely. He knew when to keep silent and when to speak. He did not reveal his feelings indiscriminately. The Bible calls all of his disciples to the expression of his life through them. It also calls us to emulate him in healthy ways of emotional expression. The scriptural exhortations are, "that Christ may be formed in you," (Galatians 4:19) and "you should follow in his footsteps," (1 Peter 2:21).

We will see how the Son of Man can enable those who are emotionally inexpressive, who I will call the cowboy and playboy, to venture forth and show their feelings. He also assists those who let their emotions run too easily to be more centered in him.

The Cowboy

The one person who best portrays the cowboy, the hero of Western folklore, is John Wayne. Sometimes he showed more tender feelings towards his horse than towards the women in his life. He was portraying a stereotype of masculinity. Not all cowboys fit the John Wayne movie image. Those who do, however, would never dream of shedding a tear or showing tenderness. The same is true of the urban cowboy. He shows little tender feeling whether he is employed in the executive suite or the factory assembly line. He is the tough guy that defies being pushed around. Such a macho orientation finds its way into home life, international politics, and interpersonal relationships. He would rather send in the Marines to subdue the enemy than bargain at the peace talks.

He is competitive. It is important for his survival that he is the fastest gun in the west. In the business world, the language of competition is "going in for the kill," "beat the competitor to the draw," and similar belligerent phrases. Even the milder forms of macho expressed in the statement "walk softly and carry a big stick" disguise aggressiveness. Such behavior may be seen as a manifestation of male hormones, but no matter how it is explained it serves to alienate people from each other.

The cowboy is prejudiced. Males who manifest emotions are called fags and sissies. The fear of being seen as a homosexual is present in many males who inhibit the more tender emotions. Certain cultural groups that are more expressive of their feelings are labelled as effeminate. The cowboy would rather die a painful death than kiss, hug, and tell another male that he loves him.

The cowboy is mystified by certain emotional needs of women. He can't understand why his wife wants to be held physically without extending the intimacy of sexual intercourse. He can't understand why women can talk for hours and hours and not get bored or go and do something recreational. He cries out, in the words of a popular song, "Why can't a woman be more like a man?" It is of interest to note that many a cowboy on reaching his midlife crisis begins to develop some of the more female characteristics like emotionality and tenderness with other people.

The Playboy

The chief characteristic of the playboy is that he treats women as "things" to be used rather than as people to be respected. The character in modern fiction who best portrays the playboy is James Bond. He is always surrounded by beautiful women but never makes a strong emotional attachment to any of them. Women are treated as sex objects, as ways to make the man look good, as conquests. They are certainly not as important as men or ambition.

The playboy is against permanent commitments. Why get trapped with one woman when so many "bunnies" are available? Sometimes the playboy syndrome comes out in a man's mid-life crisis. He feels trapped by providing for his wife, wants to affirm his sexuality with a younger woman, and generally wants to be free of the boredom of sameness.

He is insecure about himself. The middle-aged playboy adopts a more youthful style of dress. He feels poorly about his deteriorating physical condition. He exercises with the frenzy similar to that of a young woman with anorexia nervosa. His mortality creeps up on him but he denies that like all people he is heading for the grave.

The playboy dominates women. Such a posture comes out of his insecurity. He could not for one minute see a woman as his equal. In Christian circles he demands submission in the most harmful and distorted manner. I once heard a pastor in a wedding sermon say to the wife, "You should submit to your husband at all times, even if he tells you to jump over a cliff after him you should obey." Such distortion of the meaning of submission feeds into the playboy's desire to dominate.

The playboy depersonalizes women. They are deprived of their status as equal partners and turned into objects. The rules of the playboy are extremely narcissistic. He wants women to give him the world on his own terms. He becomes highly threatened when a woman thinks for herself. He sees women as girls, wives as "good women" at home. He joins all-male social clubs and fights to have women excluded from their membership. He knows little or nothing of the experience of Galatians 3:28 where in Christ "there is neither . . . male nor female."

The playboy and the cowboy are extreme examples of the inexpressive male in our culture. When we move to the other end of the spectrum of emotional expression, however, we find just as many problems in human relationships.

Uncontrolled Feelings

We now live in a culture where the expression of feeling is touted as the essence of emotional health. The advice given to the hero of the "Star Wars" epic is "Luke, trust your feelings." The "let your feelings hang out" advice is at times potentially destructive, especially for those weak in logic who have problems with emotional control. Both males as well as females suffer from this disabling disease of the mouth. Let us examine the devestating effects of emotional overexpressiveness.

A fire is not extinguished when it is doused with gasoline. Relationship problems are not solved when people shout at each other in anger. Such emotional expression actually serves to make the angry person more inflamed. Emotional ventilation only gives insight into the depth of the anger and hurt. It does not solve the problem. The advice to angry people to beat an inanimate object, like a carpet, is useless in problem solving. People cannot reason with their emotions out of control.

People who let their feelings "overrun the river banks" frighten other people into silence. In counselling I often face the dynamic of the "pursuer" and the "distancer." The more the one partner nags, the more the other partner goes into a protective shell. Relationship problems are not solved through blame. One woman told me that her husband was as "stubborn as an ox." She contributed to the relationship impasse with such repeated accusations. She had to learn more constructive ways of "holding her tongue" before the relationship improved.

The extremes of emotional expression are found in all of our lives. We all need to be liberted by Christ in either the setting free or binding of emotion. How then does this transformation take place? What models do we have of healthy and appropriate emotional expression?

Jesus—The Example

Jesus lived in another time and culture but still he is the model and power source for emotional wholeness. One of the titles he used to explain his person and ministry was Son of Man. This particular self-designation was associated with his suffering and death. The name represented his work for and identification with humankind. It also tells us that he is everything we can be as bearers of the image of God.

He is perfect person and the complete contrast of the playboy and cowboy. Jesus wept. He was tender towards children. He was concerned for his mother even in his hour of deepest suffering. He physically touched people and let even women touch him. He was compassionate towards his enemies, forgiving towards his tormentors, and believed in people despite his knowledge of their dark stream. How then can we follow in his footsteps and allow his Spirit to transform us into his image?

The transforming change is the first and essential step in the process of becoming like the Son of Man. It is known in biblical terms as the "new birth." It is a point in the process of conversion where the Spirit of God in some mystical manner takes possession of our lives. It does not result in a finished product where the person is perfectly like Christ. It is the source of power wherein we work out our salvation with fear and trembling.

It is also a process of change. We grow towards the point of healthy emotional expression. No matter how tragic a person's emotional history, he or she is still capable of emotional growth. But it is not a growth accomplished immediately. It is not a magic formula where spiritual and emotional crutches are thrown away and we dance rejoicing into the world. Despite actual instant physical healings, emotional changes usually take place over a period of time. The Scriptures are process oriented. Consider Paul's words, "I have learned (a process) to be content whatever the circumstances," (Philippians 4:11).

The process of growth involves a slow metamorphosis. Reflect for a moment on the development of the butterfly. It undergoes a slow change from the cocoon to the time it flies with new wings. We dare not speed up the process of metamorphosis. We should not cut the cocoon with a knife to help the butterfly emerge. It needs the struggle out of its grublike state to develop strength in its wings to fly. So too with our emotional development. Is is through much tribulation that we come into the kingdom. Pain and process cannot be avoided in personal growth.

The goal of change is that we become like the Son of Man. Consider for a moment the following scriptures: "I am again in the pains of childbirth until Christ is formed in you," (Galatians 4:9) and "Be transformed by the renewing of your mind," (Romans 12:2). The underlying assumption behind these verses is that we have had our minds shaped by influences alien to God. One area where our minds have been bent from their original shape is when we were prohibited certain feelings. In other areas, we let our feelings run with no control. We are exhorted to let our minds undergo a metamorphosis. We need the freedom to constructively channel all our God-given feelings.

The process of putting on the mind and character of Christ has rewards as well as dangers. It is foolish for us to try and imitate his style of living in a literal and slavish manner. The fact that he did not own property does not preclude our ownership of "things." Having his mind, however, includes a certain attitude towards possessions. We are to practice hospitality, be aware of the needs of the poor, and have a certain detachment towards possessions. Our having the mind of Christ also involves the disciplined expression of emotion.

The means of change towards the image of Christ is a lifelong task made possible by being, listening, touching and channeling.

Being

The stamp of the image of God on our lives gives us a uniqueness beyond race, education, or socioeconomic class. The new birth releases all sorts of growth possibilities for that image in us. Reflect for a moment on the advice given to parents, "Train a child in the way he should go, and when he is old he will not turn from it," (Proverbs 22:6). Another way of saying "in the way he should go" is "according to the unique personality of the child." Too often, though, that unique personality is conformed to the image of the world or the desires of a parent. One of the results of being squeezed into another's mold is emotional inexpressiveness. Take some of the messages that we get from our environment that inhibit the healthy expression of feeling:

Don't get angry, it upsets your parents.
You are acceptable if you don't express a
contrary opinion.
Girls should not compete with boys.
Boys should not play with toy dolls.

All of these statements have the potential of inhibiting the development and expression of our God-given uniqueness. It is especially true when the conforming person seeks the approval of the person who sets up conditions of worth. How then do we discover the true being of the other?

Listening

An exercise I often use in counselling with couples is to get them to declare to each other "This is who I am." I am continually surprised how people fail to see others for who they really are. There is some truth in the saying "we see what we want to see." Our needs and expectations for people condition our view of them at times.

The way we get to know others is to let them teach us about themselves. We need to suspend our preconceived judgments and let others speak as our instructor about themselves. How many times we have come away from an interpersonal situation with a feeling of dissatisfaction when the person told us:

What you should do is . . .
If I were you, I would . . .
I know exactly what you are going through . . .

The beauty of Jesus is that people felt that he idenified with them. He was nonjudgemental but still had standards. He gave commands but let people take responsibility for their lives. He knew what people had in their hearts but still believed the best for them. No wonder that people were responsive to his commands for change and growth. He could truly listen to people, warts and all, and allow their unique personalities to be shaped into a more godly image.

Touching

A popular Christian song proclaims "He touched me and made me whole." The touch of the Master in our lives comes directly through his Spirit or through other Christians.

We are aware of the touch of the Spirit in many ways. I often become aware of overpowering emotion when I am singing songs of praise with other believers. I interpret such feeling as the movement of the Spirit of God. Many times I have seen inexpressive people release emotions in such Spirit-filled worship.

Being touched by the people of God can be a transforming experience for emotionally inexpressive people. Small care-groups can help them gain the courage to admit and express a wide range of feelings.

The touch of the needy world often softens the heart and expands the person to a full expression of feeling. We meet Jesus in the margins of life—in the midst of starvation, oppression, exploitation, sexism, or racism. He is there with great concern and invites us to feel the same.

Channeling

Healing also comes when persons who suffer from emotional excess channel their feelings. Jesus had control of his feelings. There were times in his life when he refused to speak or reveal his inner feelings. He held his tongue in the face of the taunting of King Herod and his soldiers. He restrained his anger in the temple when he turned the tables over. We read that he made a whip of cords. It was a deliberate act that preceded the expression of anger. He did not just rush in wildly to chase out the traders in the temple. His anger was focused and in control. Such scriptural examples can be put to practical use in our relationships.

Many a hurtful situation can be avoided when one angry person voluntarily chooses to "cool off" before seeking to solve the problem. A time of prayer and meditation is useful to gain a realistic perspective. The Lord can literally set our hearts at peace (Philippians 4:6–7) before we attempt to resolve a situation that involves conflict. Impulse control does not come through some magical event. Controlling emotion involves conscious effort on our part. The Son of Man is our example and enabler in the control of emotion. His life within us is the power that slowly transforms us into his likeness.

A Personal Life Response

In what ways do you lack balance in the expression of emotion? Are there any emotions which present special problems in your life? What are you currently doing to bring about change in these problem areas of your emotions?

Applying the Truth

- Do you have a friend or group of friends with whom you can venture forth in the healing of your excesses or deficits of emotional expression?
- In what ways is the Spirit of Christ gently inviting you to new wholeness in emotional expression?
- In what ways do you serve as a stumbling block to others in the expression of their emotion?

The Emotionally Healthy Christian

What Do You Think?

A test of whether we are doing the will of God or not is that it is full of suffering and joylessness.	Yes	No	Maybe
Quality relationships are based on the extent to which we meet each other's needs.	Yes	No	Maybe
A prerequisite for intimacy is a strong sense of one's own identity.	Yes	No	Maybe

The Emotionally Healthy Christian

Our society expends much of its energy and time in a search for health. At some time or another each of us has tried a new health food, abstained from foods high in cholesterol content, jogged, been to an aerobic dance class, or imbibed an assortment of vitamins. The Bible encourages us in our search for health but has a focus beyond that of just physical health. The apostle Paul writes, "For physical training is of some value, but godliness has value for all things . . . ," (1 Timothy 4:8).

The term "godly" evokes all sorts of images in our minds. For some, there are memories of the burning bush and Moses. For others, the terrors of the judgements in the Book of Revelation. The more secular see godly people as pompous and holier than thou. In this chapter the godly person is viewed as emotionally healthy, the prototype of healthy humanity, the closest approximation to the prefall condition of Adam and Eve, the very likeness of Jesus Christ. Two factors stand out as we consider godly character from the perspectives of God's character and the prefall condition of our early parents: An emotionally healthy person works well and loves well.

Working Well

The emotionally healthy person is one who has a job to do and does it well. God said to Adam and Eve, "Subdue the earth," and "Be fruitful and multiply."

It is no coincidence, therefore, that when we finish a project, accomplish a goal, or put the finishing touches to our work, that we look on it and, like God, affirm that it is good.

We live in an economic climate where people are unemployed, underemployed, or working in the absence of personal fulfillment. The drudgery of such conditions stands in sharp contrast to the satisfaction of God who looked on creation and saw that it was good. A lack of fulfillment in one's work often leads to emotional breakdown. We have all been appalled at the reports of the increase of family violence in the areas of our country where unemployment is high. Contrary to popular opinion, people do not enjoy being on welfare. People generally have strong negative feelings towards themselves when they are unemployed for lengthy periods. We don't thrive personally on handouts from the government or charity. We all need fulfilling employment. It is the way we were designed by God.

What then is the definition of fulfilling work? It is certainly not a perpetual feeling of well-being since we all at some times hate getting up in the morning and going to work. Broadly defined, fulfilling work comes when we are doing the will of God. I once heard someone say that the will of God for people is where the joy of the heart and the need of the world intersect in their lives. Let us examine this perspective for a moment.

The Joy of the Heart

If the work that we do no longer represents the joy of our heart, then something is radically wrong in our lives. Thomas Carlyle, who found great contentment in his work as an author, wrote "Blessed is he who has found his work; let him ask no other blessedness." Why then do people lose the joy of doing their work?

Burnout is a popular term today applied to the weariness, cynicism and boredom felt towards work by those who have had inordinate demands placed on their system for too long. The daily hassels of life combined with threatening life events sometimes bring us to the point of exhaustion. The Lord did not design our systems to operate at such levels of stress. I remember a ditty that expresses the experience of the overworked person:

> There once was a man my grandfather knew
> Who had so many things he had to do,
> That whenever he thought it was time to begin,
> He couldn't, because of the state he was in.

When the bow is bent for too long and with too much tension, the string snaps. God did not supply us with limitless energy to be squandered in an indiscriminate fashion. The joy of our hearts can be reduced to the ashes of despair through burnout. The other extreme in our work lives is that of boredom and underuse of our abilities.

When it comes to a definition of stress, there are two types of people, turtles and racehorses. The racehorse is not happy walking around the racetrack. It was created to run. Often there is little joy in our work because we are operating below the level of our ability. This may be due to a loss of a job, ignorance and underuse of our true abilities, or a willful burying of our talents in the ground (Matthew 25:25). The person in Jesus' story mismanaged his gifts and reported to the master his fear of even beginning the task. Fear kills the adventure of living. The turtle, by contrast, was not created to keep up with the racehorse. It is important for the turtles of life to pace themselves well in work and relationships and not feel guilty when they don't meet the expectations of the racehorses in their lives. The quest for fulfillment in our work requires that we balance the pace of our work with our physical capabilities.

The joy of the heart is not necessarily expressed in a subjective happiness, but rather it is an objective blessedness—the word that Jesus used in the Sermon on the Mount. Jesus also expressed the essence of this word when he set the parameters for the servant spirit in the upper room. He told the disciples, "Now that you know these things, you will be blessed if you do them," (John 13:17). A blessed person is one who stands in God's favor. We do not earn this favor but our response to it is one of obedience. Sometimes obedience leads to trouble in this world. It led the Son of Man to his crucifixion. We too find ourselves in opposition to the systems of the world. As we attempt to liberate ourselves and others from these systems the personal fulfillment is great but persecution, misunderstanding, and rejection hurts. The "well done good and faithful servant" is our joy. In the next section we will see how this joy is connected to the need of the world.

The Need of the World

The world is both a needy and a greedy place. A fulfilling and joyful work is responsive to need and does not reinforce greed.

Personal greed is one of the more subtle sins of humankind. But it enslaves all its followers. Greed works against emotional health whether in personal or international affairs. At the individual level, we jostle our neighbor in the supermarket when there is a butter shortage or we hide needed text books in the university library so others can't earn a good grade. At the political level, greed causes us to exploit Central American nationals through the use of cheap labor, and to supply arms to rightest governments to keep our consumptive lifestyle going.

What then is the difference between greed and need? Are we not more prone to judge ourselves needy and others greedy? Consider some guidelines that the Bible sets forth:

- What does it mean that God will supply our needs? (Matthew 6:25–34)
- Why are we encouraged to look to the needs of others rather than to our own? What example do we have? (Philippians 2)

- What are the implications in the Lord's prayer contained in the words "Give us today our daily bread"?
- What are our responsibilities towards the needs of other nations on earth?

A job well done is therefore responsive to the need of humankind and evokes the joy of the heart. It is also a job to be shared with other people. God did not give Adam a job to do and then isolate him from his marriage partner Eve. We are not fulfilled if we carry out our calling in life in some remote cave. Emotional health is to be found in relationships. Innately we all long for intimate relationships.

Loving Well

The Lord created us for relationship. The image of God stamped on our lives destines us for fulfillment in relationship. "Male and female he created them" means that emotional health depends to a large extent on healthy interpersonal relationships.

Intimacy and Not Isolation

People wrapped up in themselves make small and miserable packages. Social isolation in its more extreme forms is found in persons with severe mental disorders. One disorder manifests itself in almost total withdrawal from contact with the outside world. A less severe problem is shyness. Countless shy people seek help such as assertiveness training to try and secure more productive ways of interacting with the world. Shyness stems from a lack of confidence in or knowledge of one identity. Psychologist Erik Erikson explains in his theory of personal development that the task of adolescence is to discover personal identity. Unless people successfully navigate adolescence and emerge with a good sense of identity, they find it difficult to find intimacy in their early twenties.

The Bible presents relationship as the evidence of the image of God. Think of the last time that you felt content to the depths of your being. Was it not in the context of a relationship where the person listened, cared, and treated you as a unique person? There are certain things that are needed in a relationship that contribute towards intimacy. The next section is an elaboration of some of these qualities of a good relationship.

From Need to Choice

Needy persons can be dangerous persons in human relationships. In some ways they are like the proverbial bucket in the song "There's a hole in the bucket, dear Liza." The hole keeps the bucket empty. There are many manifestations of such neediness in our society. Take the bondage under which many single people find themselves. It comes from the philosophy that says "you can't be a complete person unless you are married." The latter is especially true in the case of single women in the church. Terms like "Mr. Right," "the other half," and tales such as Cindarella and Sleeping Beauty condition single persons to think that they are incomplete without a marriage partner. The result is that people feel guilty about career aspirations, get married for the wrong reasons, and generally want another to fill up the need in their lives. They go around like a Pac-Man gobbling up dots in relationships and never find themselves to be completed circles.

Loneliness needs can be met through intimate same and opposite sex friendships. Many people avoid such friendships out of the fear of rejection. Past hurts, often with their parents, condition lonely people to build protective walls around their lives. The cure for such a condition of isolation involves the experience of God's acceptance through another person. Such a process involves risk-taking on the part of the lonely person. Some find it easier to take risks in a care group in their church or in the context of a caring relationship with a counsellor. "The turtle only makes progress when it sticks its neck out," so the saying goes. Hurts of the past that condition loneliness must be dealt with before we can experience productive relationships. We cannot enter a relationship with the expectation that it will compensate entirely for unmet needs of the past that arose out of rejection.

Recently I counselled with a man who was seeking a divorce after only a few years of marriage. His wife was an attractive, supportive, and intelligent woman, however, he complained that she was not able to meet "all" his needs. When I asked the nature of these needs, I became aware that he was asking too much from his wife. He had been so rejected by his parents that his need for affirmation was like a bottomless pit that could never be filled by one person. He was asking the impossible from his marriage. After a period of individual counselling, he had the courage to deal with the rejections of the past. There was a slow process of personal healing that began to impact his marriage. He began to relate to his wife out of choice and not need.

Reflect for a moment on the nature of God. There is no neediness within the Godhead. Father, Son, and Holy Spirit exist in perfect fellowship yet each one has an identity. God did not create the world out of need, but choice, to express the Godhead in creation. A healthy human relationship comes from the posture of "I choose you" rather than "I need you." Healthy relationships therefore reflect the health and completeness of the persons who make up the union.

A Light Not a Mirror

We often read of people described in terms such as "the president's daughter," the "minister's wife," or other ways that enmesh the identity of one person in that of another. Children of famous parents, siblings with popular brothers and sisters, and all who must play second fiddle to another battle to establish their own identity. The Bible does not say that God created Adam and his wife. Her name was Eve. A name reflected an identity. She was the mother of all living. She was not just Adam's other half. She had a light of her own and was not just a mirror image of her husband.

We are not just carbon copies of each other. The apostle Paul described the church as a body with varied parts. (1 Corinthiams 12:12–26) It is important that our identities are not eclipsed by those of others.

A "Hands Off" Approach

The experience of relationship implies a certain degree of connectedness with each other. A healthy relationship is where one person does not "lord it over" the other. The issue of control often occupies a lot of negative energy in relationships. Our insecurity causes us to have a controlling "hands on" approach to those we love. The most asked question in seminars that I conduct on the rearing of children is "What sort of discipline should I use with my children?" A more effective "hands off" approach asks the question "How can I teach my child to take responsibility in life?" We encounter great insecurity in the process of letting our children go. Such uneasiness on the part of parents has its root in a spirit of fear. We fear the dangers of drugs, the marring of our reputation as parents, and the thought that our children will reject us like we rejected our own parents.

A "hands off" approach to relationships involves letting the other person take responsibility for his or her own life. An environment that models responsible living, allows children to learn from their mistakes and successes, and communicates the message "I trust you to make the right decision," is one where we can become all that God intended us to be. Consider for a moment:

- Does the Lord grant us the freedom to fail?
- How can we look to the best interest of the other with a "hands off" posture towards them?

All the parameters of a good relationship can be summed up with one biblical word, *covenant*. Let us now examine this frequently misunderstood word.

Covenants and Contracts

Human relationships can be directed by covenants or controlled by contracts. Contracts are a familiar part of all our lives. Often I wonder why my word is not good enough in the sale of a house. Why sign a contract? It is precisely because the other party wants to protect a series of personal rights. The contract is a binding legal document that protects people from the exploitation of broken promises. Now a covenant is also an agreement, however, it is qualitatively different from a contract. In a covenant I look to the best interests of the other. In a contract I protect my own interests.

Today, marriages, friendships, and other relationship commitments are treated more like contracts. The emphasis is on personal gain. People are evaluated in terms of their contribution to our personal fulfillment. Marriage partners are chosen according to their ability to exchange services. We speak of a person as a "good catch" if they come to the relationship with power, sexual attractiveness, or money. The relationship is in trouble when the service is no longer needed or provided. The "until death us do part" component is missing. Contracts are only "for better." Covenants are "for better or for worse."

God set the pattern for covenants, "I will be your God and you will be my people." Nothing shall separate his people from his love. All his goodness is at our disposal. God's covenant is an eternal commitment to his people.

A healthy human relationship is characterized by a covenant bond between two or more people. There is great security in knowing that others are committed to us "warts and all." They will not walk out on us when we behave like a brat. We will not be left stranded when we grow old or sickly and lose our physical attractiveness. We will not be dumped when we lose our service value. Yet, the covenant bond is not license for us to live out our dark stream in our relationships. At times, we wear our covenantal relationships threadbare through our irresponsible behavior. Personal commitments become strained, tempers flare up and patience runs short in these times of personal failure. A covenant, however, is a foundation on which many a hurt relationship can be rebuilt. All avenues of reconciliation and forgiveness need to be explored before the relationship is sacrificed for the health of the individual.

The glue in human relationships is not passion but commitment. We define our lives together by our past commitments not our present needs or future hopes. Sometimes in the midst of the hard grind of life relationships lose their passion. It is at this point that love is based on a decision and not a feeling. Where would we be with God if he said, "If you love me, then I will be your God"? Such conditional love is based on a contract of personal interest and not a covenant.

Our commitments need constant renewal. In a covenant relationship, we actively seek the best interests of the other person. I once heard a person say that the true spelling of love was "time". We need to give time to listen to and nurture those to whom we have given our commitment. The Lord admonishes us not to neglect "to meet together." What the Lord says of church commitments may also be said of marriage. A marriage dies through neglect. If some people put as little work into their businesses as they do into their marriages they would be financially bankrupt.

The heart of commitment is actively working for the best interests of the other. A covenant involves giving ourselves to the task of encouraging the other person to be all that God intended that person to be. Such love means not trying to squeeze people into the mold of our personal agenda for their lives. It means a concern for their freedom—which involves risk. When we grant our children freedom, we risk letting them make mistakes. When we are concerned for the best interests of our spouse we risk their growth. Yet, the benefits of growth far outweigh the safety of stagnation. The oil that insures the smooth running of a covenant is that "it is more blessed to give than to receive." In a world of takers that is a radical concept.

Applying the Truth

- When and under what circumstances did you last feel that you were a part of a job well done?
- What are some of your options if you are feeling some degree of burnout in your employment?
- What are some of the factors that make for quality relationships in your life?
- Can you characterize your present vocation as one where you experience joy as you meet the need of the world?
- Evaluate your current relationships from the perspective of either covenants or contracts.

Questions About Passion

Questions About Passion

1. *Why do people experience pain in emotional expression?*

Sometimes we put on tough exteriors to hide inner tenderness or hurt. On other occasions we are given the message by certain churches and religious leaders that passion is an unspiritual part of our being. We are told to bridle our passions at all costs. We are to bring them under the rule of "correct thinking."

Some people are prohibited in their family of origin in the expression of certain feelings. The result is often loneliness and confusion. I once had a patient describe her father as a "person so cut off from his feelings that he seemed like a total stranger to me."

Others are afraid to express their emotion because they have seen the devastating consequences of emotionality in their home environment. One patient told me "I will never show my feelings of anger because my father had such an uncontrolled temper."

The central thrust of this book is that emotions are to be acknowledged and appropriately expressed. The consciousness raising experience of identification with "persons of like passion" in the Bible can begin to set us free towards personal wholeness.

2. *What defenses do people commonly use against emotional expression?*

I have often heard emotionally defensive persons described as "tough on the outside with well-hidden soft hearts." Persons afraid of their passions build up unique systems of defense often called masks. Some of our masks include our desperate attempts to please or placate others. Other defenses include various ways of blaming others. "The devil made me do it" is a lame excuse that we use to escape personal responsibility for our actions.

We also cover up our fears with a saccharine sweet spirituality that praises the Lord outwardly while we cry in desperation on the inside. I once heard a person describe such inauthentic religiosity as "cloud nine dishonesty" where with pride the person claims "I had the baptism of the Spirit and all my anxious and negative feelings went away." There are no instant solutions to most of the hurts of life.

We need to note that there are times when it is healthy to restrain the expression of passion. Sometimes, it is destructive to wear our feelings on our sleeves.

3. *How can emotion be tempered by rationality?*

Philosophers from many faiths have warned of the danger of uncontrolled passion. The writer of the ancient Hindu proverb said, "Conquer your passions and you conquer the whole world." Alexander Pope wrote, "What reason weaves, by passion is undone."

What then is the place of passion in our lives? Some saints are inclined to feel their religion and they are criticized by the rationalists as being too emotional. Some center on the question, "Is it correct?" Some operate on the premise "better felt than telt." A more immediate and subjective experience of God is their quest.

The solution to the human dilemma of feeling versus thinking is not to get rid of the fantastic and stick to the realistic. Various psychological techiques that help patients explore their past convince me that there are some pretty shady characters living in the house of reason. These characters that lurk in the dark recesses of our mind represent our human sinfulness. Pure and unadulterated reason does not always drive humans to action. Personal and social biases also direct our actions. "God told me" is never an unbiased statement on our part.

The balance of emotion and thought is essential for the healthy expression of our faith and person. The worship of the Lord in "Spirit and truth" in dynamic balance is the expression of personal wholeness. It is of interest to note that the biblical term "know" includes more than head knowledge. When the Bible says that Adam knew his wife Eve, it is speaking of their communion through sexual intercourse. It certainly does not mean that they sat and discussed the technical aspects of the sexual relationship. In no way, therefore, can either fact or feeling be given priority in healthy Christians.

4. *How can passion and reason coexist as equal partners?*

People have given their lives for the truths they believe in their minds. Yet, dry orthodoxy hardly inspires martyrs. The Martin Luthers of the Reformation and Civil Rights movement were passionate in their defense of the truth.

It is passion that helps people build cathedrals, paint the roof of the Sistine Chapel, compose hymns, and respond to the needs of the poor and oppressed.

In both the Golden Era of Greece and the Renaissance of Europe, sculptors intended their figures to depict truth and order, but they did not exclude passion. The eyes of many of these works of art were often dilated. Passion energizes rationality. The other side of the coin is that passion needs to be disciplined by rationality.

A healthy human experience involves the delicate balance between thoughts and emotions. The "hot heads" in our midst need to be tempered with some rationality. The rationalists need to listen at times to their feelings. We are, after all, persons with two cerebral hemispheres. The left side of the brain helps us operate at the level of logic and rationality. The right side of the brain assists us in our intuitions and feelings.

5. *What about the times when a situation does not feel right to us? Can we trust our feelings in such circumstances?*

Again we need to strive for a balance. There are those who feel that we can solve most human problems if we try harder to think in a logical manner. Such conclusions render a gross injustice to the intuitive side of people. A woman friend of mine once told me of a problematic situation she and other members of the church tried to solve. She was told to abandon her emotional way of solving and submit to the male leadership's rational approach. Throughout the event she reported that she had uneasy feelings about their conclusions. Somehow things "did not fit." In the end her intuitive assessment of the situation proved to be correct.

We need to learn new ways to trust and monitor our

feelings. After all, the "Spirit bearing witness with our spirits" is an emotional experience that sometimes defies human logic. Persons of like passion in the Bible let feelings and thoughts direct their actions. We follow in their footsteps.

6. *What about the times in my life when my feelings seem dead?*

We all pass through dark periods in our lives when numbness overtakes our feelings. We experience such dry spells when God seems far removed from our lives. We simply cannot feel our religion. The old formulas given to us in the high days of our religious experience simply do not work. Everything from praying in tongues to praise songs at the worship service does not restore our feeling of peace and joy. What is wrong with a person in the midst of such emotional flatness? The answer may be that God is teaching the person to rely on him apart from feelings.

Too often we seek emotional highs in our religion like the alcoholic who looks for feelings from the bottle. The addict lives off the feelings derived from the drugs. Some Christians are addicted to the feelings generated from the practice of their faith. If we love feelings for their own sake, we have departed from our love for God. Our quest is for God and not for the feelings derived from religious experience. Our faith is in him and not changing human passion or even great logical theories and ideas. God may not be emotionally felt during the dry spells of the soul but that does not mean that he has abandoned us. We need to be less attached to the feelings that derive from our walk of faith, and more focused on God himself.